Knee Deep in Montana's Trout Streams

Also by John Holt

Waist Deep in Montana's Lakes
Reel Deep in Montana's Rivers
All About Trout
Chasing Fish Tales
Kicking Up Trouble
Montana Fly Fishing Guide–West
Montana Fly Fishing Guide–East
Madison River—River Journal Series

Knee Deep in Montana's Trout Streams

Second Edition

John Holt

PRUETT PUBLISHING COMPANY
BOULDER, COLORADO

Some of the information in this book originally appeared in different form in the following publications: *The Angling Report, Fly Fisherman, Flyfishing, Rocky Mountain Game & Fish,* and *Trout.*

Printed in the United States
10   9   8   7   6   5   4   3   2   1

Library of Congress Cataloging-in-Publication data

Holt, John, 1951–
    Knee deep in Montana's trout streams / John Holt. — 2nd ed.
       p.   cm.
    Includes index.
    ISBN 0-87108-886-X (pb)
    1. Trout fishing—Montana—Guidebooks. 2. Fly fishing—Montana—Guidebooks. 3. Rivers—Montana—Guidebooks. 4. Montana—Guidebooks. I. Title.
SH688.U6H65   1996
799.1'755—DC20   96-44763
                                              CIP

Cover design by Mike Signorella, Signorella Graphics
Interior book design by Kathleen McAffrey, Starr Design
Cover and interior photographs by John Holt except where noted otherwise.

For those who have stuck by me

Contents

When I was younger I could remember anything, whether it happened or not; but my faculties are decaying now and soon I shall be so I cannot remember any but the things that never happened. It is sad to go to pieces like this but we all have to do it.

Mark Twain
The Autobiography of Mark Twain

Acknowledgments

Certainly this book would not have been possible without the help and input from the following people, but it would just as certainly have been a lesser entity. My thanks go out to my good friend Tony Acerrano; Steve Shimek of Travel Montana; The Montana Department of Fish, Wildlife and Parks, including Pat Clancey, Steve Leathe, Dick Oswald, Scott Rumsey, Jim Vashro, and Tom Weaver; Tom Rosenbauer at Orvis; Don Causey; John Randolph; and the many guides and outfitters around Montana who took the time to show me their favorite streams.

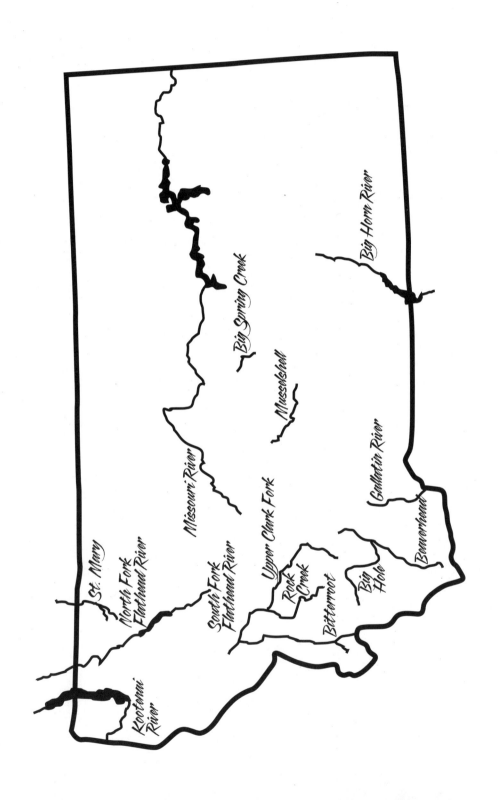

Introduction:
Madman's Mecca

*M*ontana has dominated my thinking since a fishing trip in the Gallatin valley in the sixties. I used to hang out in the North Woods of Wisconsin, but after a decade or so I grew tired of the summer tourists, the over-fished lakes, and the places called "Whispering Pines Bar and Grill." (I do still occasionally miss the fishing around Cornucopia and the bar in Presque Isle, but that's life.) So when a sports editor position opened up in northwestern Montana, I quit the paper in Wisconsin and U-hauled my act West into the promised land of the Big Sky state. The fact that my job at the daily did not last very long was a mixed blessing that turned me loose on the state's trout waters with an aggression and enthusiasm that rages away today as strong as ever.

If someone casually mentioned that large, steelhead-like rainbows were swimming in the tailwaters of the Missouri River below Fort Peck Dam surrounded by the surreal badlands in this sparsely populated corner of the state, I hopped in my pickup and drove there— immediately, if not sooner.

Lynda, my ex-wife, would wave goodbye, secure in the knowledge that sometimes I would return with good Kodachrome shots of trout fishing, sometimes I would round up assignments related to the trip, and sometimes (much rarer) I would actually receive a check for my efforts.

But most often, the few photos suitable for angling articles were mixed in with countless scenes of people standing in front of places like the Ranger Bar in Dupuyer, cattle blocking the road in middle-of-nowhere eastern Montana, and curious exposures that defied explanation or description.

The true story is that fly fishing rapidly passes through stages beginning with mere interest, progressing to avocation, then addiction, and ending with oblivion.

Every time I turn around, I hear tales of a great, new undiscovered angling nirvana: Big browns finning away in some minuscule creek near the ghost town of Bannack. Golden trout in some pristine, alpine setting just down the road. World-record rainbows in a little spring creek out behind Sumatra.

What you never hear about are the trophy mosquitoes that provide some of the finest pass shooting in North America, rattlesnakes that curl around your legs, ranchers guarding their property rights with bazookas, and streambeds that last saw water when Lewis and Clark were out here trying to figure out what to do with Great Falls. It's all fine sport to me. I love a wild goose chase. I see it as metaphor for the larger business of living—but catching trout is fun, too. Every once in a while, when one of those bizarre tips actually turns out to be real, life becomes a piscatorial epiphany.

There was the time a guy told me through his whiskey, "You take a left off the highway at Winnett (don't get your hopes up, even if this was the actual town, you'd never find the creek) and drive 7.9 miles down the goddamned gravel road until you hit a shot-to-hell stop sign. I was the bastard that shot it. Hang a left for a quarter-mile and stop at a wooden bridge. I built the sucker in '51. Pull over and walk up to that jacked-around beaver dam. Hell, there's browns for miles up from it. Yeah. Damn good fishin', but keep an eyeball cocked for that pack of wild dogs over there."

I was gone before sunset, parked at the bridge by dawn, and flinging Woolly Buggers tight to a brushy bank as the sun jumped up red and hot. Damn! were there brown trout in this stream! Every cast turned a fish: one pound, two pounds, twenty inches. No dogs, though. Man, I could do an article on this.

After a couple of days of bliss, I went back home and got on the phone to my fishing buddy in Missoula. He said that he already knew about the water and that if I ever wrote even one word about it to anyone including family members, he'd come up to Whitefish (where I live) and break my legs and all of my fly rods. Well, good friends are a rare commodity, and I love my fly rods—and my legs—quite a bit, so that stream is still a secret waiting to be leaked.

And that's why Montana is home. That kind of experience can take place every day of the year (if you don't mind freezing to death once in a while). There is so much good trout water in Montana that spending a lifetime checking it all out would be, at best, a small beginning. It is not physically or mentally possible to sample all of the unheard-of and unfished territory in this state. Just exploring the major rivers like the Missouri, Big Hole, Clark Fork, Kootenai, and Bitterroot would take numerous lifetimes. The entertainment these venerated liquid situations provide goes far beyond casting to good numbers of big fish.

Eagles, deer, elk, sandhill cranes, and grizzlies are often spotted along these waters, and I've even stumbled across a bunch of interesting people, some of whom were actually sane. Watching a river cruise, swirl, and bubble to its own tune is usually more than enough entertainment for those of us flirting with terminal brain fade.

Finally, there are days that are pure and simple magic that happen along for no particular reason and are a result of nothing I've done. They're just there and I frequently wander through a large portion of one before realizing what's going on. Like the day that was spread out before me in the shadow of the wild Rocky Mountain Front on the high plains east of the Continental Divide. I was catching fat cutthroat trout on cast after Royal Wulff cast under a sky that was so perfectly blue it was scary. After a couple of hours I'd reached my angling fill of this aquatic banquet. Sitting on the tailgate of my pickup with the mountains blasting away into the bright light and this stream jumping to its well-rehearsed tune, I thought, damn straight, that's what this game is all about.

The North Fork of the Flathead River.

North Fork of the Flathead River

I yanked the steering wheel hard right and slammed on the brakes, the truck's front tires coming to rest uncomfortably close to the edge of a precipice falling a hundred feet to an emerald-clear river below. A heavily burdened logging truck, bound for the Plum Creek timber mill in Columbia Falls, screamed past in a cloud of red-brown dust, oblivious to our presence and near demise.

This was the infamous North Fork Road. After ten miles of paved bliss it gives way to a rugged gravel surface that continually narrows as it bumps, grinds, and careens its way north to the Canadian border. Signs at the end of the pavement and at the western exit of Glacier National Park near Camas Creek inform the unwary that they are traveling here at their own risk and should make an effort to "stay alert" if survival is of any pressing interest.

The North Fork of the Flathead River begins in the mountains that form a portion of the British Columbia and Alberta boundary, some fifty miles north of the border. Grizzly bears, black bears, gray wolves, bald eagles, lynx, ptarmigan, porcupines, possibly mountain caribou, bull trout, and westslope cutthroat trout thrive in the drainage's heavily timbered acres. Many of these species are on threatened or endangered lists.

My companion (a journalist friend from southern Florida) and I got out of the truck and drank a couple of beers while waiting for the thick dust cloud to settle. A windless dry July day coupled with a blazing logging truck often means a wait of several beers before it is safe to venture on.

The river flowed quietly and swiftly far below us, and the rise rings of large fish, probably migrating bull trout, could be seen in a quiet eddy off to one side of the main current. Upstream, a portion of the bank slumped into the river, taking a fifty-foot tree with it. The pine bobbed once in the current before disappearing beneath the water's surface. I tried to imagine its path and was rewarded with the sight of the tree popping up like a cork a couple of hundred yards downstream.

Two of Montana's native salmonids, westslope cutthroat trout and bull trout, are found in the river. The cutthroat hide behind rocks and boulders and beneath logjams all year long; the bull trout migrate from Flathead Lake fifty miles to the south. At twenty-eight miles long and ten miles wide, the body of water is the largest natural fresh-water lake west of the Mississippi and is a superb pristine environment for these fish.

The first time I caught a bull trout in the North Fork was after days of standing knee-deep (or deeper) in the cold flow casting a large Spruce Fly on a weighted line that was further handicapped with several split shot. This rig was ungainly and extremely difficult to work, even with an eight-weight rod, but it was the only way to sink the streamer down along the bottom of the deceptively powerful river. Bull trout feed extensively on other fish that hang out in the benthic currents well below the surface. I've caught fish that have disgorged a half-dozen whitefish during release attempts. They'll eat other trout, perch, sculpins—anything. They seem to come out of nowhere and strike with a sudden swiftness and power that is impressive to feel.

After about 10,000 casts and several stripping retrieves, I'd become hypnotized by the river and the casting. The pain in my shoulder was now an accepted companion. The scenery was great. Suddenly the line stopped in mid-retrieve. I figured I was snagged on the bottom. I pumped the rod a couple of unyielding times, but nothing happened.

A North Fork bull trout.

All at once the line ripped across and downstream, the reel's drag screeching away. For the next twenty minutes I hopped, staggered, and lurched down the bank, tripping over beached logs and my own feet as I frantically tried to keep up with the fish, which I assumed was a bull trout. Only a brief flash well beneath the surface so far.

I really did not want to break this one off. To not see a fish of obvious size and strength would be disappointing, to put it mildly. Eventually the bull trout tired and came to the surface about thirty feet from me. I was stunned. The fish was huge: thirty inches at least and thick, colored dull olive and silver with orange spots. What a fish! I was so shaky I could barely walk.

Slowly working the fish to me, now on its side, I lifted the rod back behind me. The trout slid toward my knees (I was by now kneeling in an unconscious form of angling supplication, I guess). The mangled Spruce Fly was tucked into the corner of the fish's mouth. When

I pushed the fly back into the trout's mouth with my fingers, several of the many teeth there drew blood. I held the fish by the tail and belly, gently working it in the still water until the creature swam out of sight. I looked at the leader (1X); it was frayed. The fly was hammered. That was enough for one day, so I went home.

Since that incident I've done some research on the species and have discovered that bull trout are closely related to the anadromous Dolly Varden but are differentiated by such things as mandibular pores and gill raker morphology. They tend to run larger than Dolly Varden and are strictly freshwater animals. In addition to devouring other fish, they will also eat mice, frogs, ducklings, bridge pilings, and abandoned Studebakers.

Bull trout inhabit clear, cold lakes and streams in Montana, Idaho, Utah, British Columbia, Alberta, and the Northwest Territories. In the lower forty-eight states, Montana has the most and the best habitat, and much of that lies in the northwest corner of the state. The Flathead River drainage extending into Canada, the western edge of Glacier National Park, and the Bob Marshall Wilderness Complex is considered to be prime turf for the fish. (Relatives are also found finning away in China, Japan, Siberia, and Korea.)

The fish is a long-distance spawner by freshwater standards, often covering over 150 miles from Flathead Lake into the tiny tributaries in British Columbia. Movement begins in late April and lasts through early summer, with much of the distance covered during spring runoff in very high, turbid conditions. Spawning takes place from September through November on gravel redds constructed in areas of good flow. Spotting a twenty-pound fish lying in ten inches of water in a stream less than fifteen feet wide is quite a sight. The fish rarely spawn before they are four or five years old and deposit an average of 1,000 eggs per pound of body weight. No one has been able to pin down a consistent spawning pattern for the fish.

"Bull trout are an anomaly in the trout world," said state fisheries biologist Pat Clancey. "Some fish spawn each year, some every other year and some less frequently than that. And some of the fish don't move back downstream until late winter or early spring of the next year. The same is true of juvenile fish. Some stay in the stream for a couple of years. Others move just after one year. No one really knows for sure what triggers the movement."

Several years ago the Montana Department of Fish, Wildlife and Parks (MDFWP) closed the season on fishing for bull trout in all but two waters west of the Continental Divide. This was brought on by surveys that revealed drastic reductions in the number of bull trout and spawning redds. Instead of addressing the problems that actually caused this precipitous decline—logging, development, pollution, etc.—the department chose to penalize fly fishermen, a constituency that has little if any impact on the fishery. In fact, fly fishermen tend to devote and contribute large sums of their time and money to preserve a threatened resource. Closing the season on bull trout eliminates the opportunity for anglers across the country to experience these magnificent creatures. I still fish for the bulls even though it's illegal. Other fly fishermen I know do, too. We like to connect with the species once or twice a year. To hell with inane regulations.

The most difficult aspect of fishing bull trout is finding them, because they often move many miles a day. Where they were one day is not likely to be a good location the next. The bull trout love the sanctity of deep water, and sinking a streamer down deep and keeping it there is something of a problem. They only way I've ever found the fish in the North Fork is to talk to fish and game people and those few hardy souls who live there. Then I spend several days moving up and down the river exploring various runs and pools. It is definitely a hit-or-miss proposition.

"Fishing for bull trout reminds me a lot of steelhead fishing," said Tony Acerrano, field editor for *Sports Afield.* "You make countless casts over the same water until you get the fly in front of a willing fish."

One thing I appreciate about this arcane experience is that nobody expects you to be successful, especially with a flyrod. Most of my friends find my obsession with bull trout to be a benign form of madness. Unlike, say, fishing the Henry's Fork, where you are expected to catch healthy numbers of big fish in order to maintain your standing as an angler, forays along the North Fork are viewed as outings conceived in failure—my kind of outing.

Because the rivers that bull trout use as travel corridors to and from their spawning grounds are big, swift, and deep, holding water will often take on the dimensions of a small pond. Large, swirling eddies deliver an assortment of food to the resting fish, and it often takes hours to work a streamer adequately through this water. Once a large Muddler Minnow of mine drifted under a pile of bleached snags down deep into the darkness. On the first strip the pattern was nailed, and the line quivered with the shaking of the bull trout's head. Each time I applied some force the trout just moved farther back under the jam. The leader parted with the Muddler, and I never saw the fish.

In many respects bull-trout chasing is like life: a lot of time and effort invested in few tangible results. One develops an appreciation for the more sophisticated aspects of our sport such as sore muscles, damp clothing, and shattered tackle and fantasies.

Fishing the North Fork is a quick study in respect for the power of mountain-generated rivers. Kayakers and other boaters have frequently misjudged the strength of the current, only to capsize and turn up drowned miles downriver. A friend of mine had the frightening experience of being sucked under by a large whirlpool while kayaking one spring. The only trace of her was the top of her paddle rotating perpendicular with the current. The river eventually spit her out, unconscious and near death, into the main flow, where she was fished out by anxious friends.

On the North Fork that July day, we looked to the west, where larch, lodgepole, and fir covered the slopes to the distant horizon. The sides of Huckleberry Mountain in Glacier National Park on the east are still recovering from the brutal fires of 1910 and 1927. Patches of dirty snow clung to shaded areas at the bottoms of avalanche chutes.

Grizzlies hold a banquet of sorts in late summer and early fall when the mountain's namesake provides a lush crop of huckleberries for the bears to gorge on with a fast-approaching winter encouraging prodigious appetites into an aggressive feeding frenzy. Huckleberry Mountain was no place to be at this time of the year unless an individual wanted to be a meat side dish at a fruitful banquet. The bears were present by the dozens, romping and crashing their several-hundred-pound bodies through the dense underbrush.

We climbed back in the truck and bounced our way up the road toward Polebridge, home of the Polebridge Mercantile, the Northern Lights Saloon, a youth hostel, and several permanent residences.

To the east, the spectacular peaks of the Livingston Range ripped into the dark blue sky, and clusters of cumulus clouds drifted in and out of the grays, reds, purples, and ochres of the mountains. A green carpet of pine stretched from the river to timberline. My friend muttered, "God, unbelievable," as he tried to absorb the view.

Then we coursed through a series of sectional clearcuts in a thick stand of lodgepole. Slash and other debris were left in ugly piles along the road and around the logged sites.

"Jesus Christ! Who lets people get away with this crap?" my friend shouted.

It was a long story that I told parts of during the rest of the drive to Polebridge. Much of the cutting is on private land, and because Montana does not have a forest practices act, owners can pretty much do as they please. On the North Fork, the U.S. Forest Service (USFS) Flathead Forest Plan proposes to log all but a few of the critical drainages that are some of the best bull trout and cutthroat trout spawning areas in the world. This activity would drastically increase the amount of sediment in the streams, in many cases producing a nearly 100 percent mortality rate in emerging fry, effectively wiping out entire populations of fish. The "timber harvest" would also eliminate the few remaining stands of old-growth trees in the area, removing travel corridors for the grizzly and wolf, reducing nesting sites for eagles and pileated woodpeckers, and destroying the view of the White-fish Range for visitors in Glacier Park.

Other problems reveal why Glacier is considered our most threat-ened national park. Oil and gas exploration abounds on the park's borders. On the North Fork, an exploratory well completed by the CENEX Corporation near Polebridge is in prime grizzly habitat and not far from nesting eagles. Just seven air miles north of the border a mammoth open pit coal mine proposal is dragged out into the open like a dead animal every now and then by a Canadian conglomerate. This operation, to be located at Cabin Creek in the North Fork drainage, is like the one now in existence at Line Creek a few miles farther north where settling ponds failed recently, sending thousands of tons of mine waste and slurry into nearby creeks. A similar disas-ter on the North Fork would spell the end of a pristine river—one pro-tected by the Wild and Scenic Rivers Act.

The two of us were marginally depressed from this discussion when we turned off the main road for the brief dusty drive to Pole-bridge, population less than 100 and not climbing. Five signs aligned along the road in Burma Shave style read, "Inconsiderate sons of bitches throw their beer cans in the ditches. Burma Shave."

The bright red façade of the Merc stood out in the midday sun. An American flag hung limply from the top of a tall wooden pole. There was one battered old pickup parked in front of the place, and a dog lay comatose in the dust behind a pair of archaic gas pumps. We went inside and bought some warm beer and beef jerky. Mounts of a vari-ety of animals found in the area hung from the walls.

There is no electricity up here (except that provided by gas-pow-ered generators), and most of the phones are of the radio variety and subject to the vagaries of atmospheric disturbances. Life here is hard in some ways for the permanent residents. The winters are long and cold, the road is a bitch to drive 99 percent of the time, and the iso-lation can be a killer. Parents with school-age children must move back down to the Flathead Valley because there aren't any schools in the North Fork (and a three-hour drive to and from town each day in January's sub-zero temperatures has little appeal). But those who live here cherish their existence. They guard this lifestyle fiercely and are cautious around outsiders. They stay here for the scenery, the wildlife, the silence, and the unbelievable freedom of it all.

The Northern Lights Saloon was closed, which was normal. I've been up this way on hundreds of trips, and it has been open only a handful of times. It does offer a surprisingly cosmopolitan selection of beers and a few brands of wine; refrigeration is provided by a cooler filled with ice. A couple of years back a fire started by a careless logger in the Red Meadow Creek area destroyed tens of thousands of acres of forest and nearly incinerated this venerable institution. The survival of this log cabin structure is a cause for celebration among confirmed derelicts everywhere.

We turned back onto the dusty, rutted road, the temperature over ninety and the sky now cloudless. Thirty minutes of cruising through a pine tree corridor and we turned west onto a smaller dirt road that paralleled a clear creek pouring over a rock and gravel bed.

A couple more miles and we pulled over, shouldered day packs, and grabbed pack rods before setting out on a well used game trail down to the creek. Three-toed woodpeckers raised a ruckus as we neared the stream, screeching as they fluttered from snag to snag, and hoary marmots could be heard whistling on the distant scree-covered slopes. A soft breeze lessened the impact of a white-hot sun. At the creek, one of the few open to fishing in the drainage (the rest are closed to protect spawning fish), we dropped down on our stomachs and drank our fill of ice-cold water that had a faint taste of pine and snow. This was not the best time of day to be fishing, but an early crop of grasshoppers was providing some gourmandish entertainment for several cutthroats along a pool that hugged the far bank.

We rigged just one flyrod and took turns casting to the rises with a hopper. All that was required was a reasonably accurate effort of twenty feet or so that landed within a foot or a yard of the bank. If we got real fancy, maybe a loop or two of slack was mended in for cosmetic purposes. The fish didn't care. Drag or no drag, the trout came readily to the fly with splashing takes before streaking to the stream's bottom to fight the tension of the line with short feisty runs. Most of the cutthroats were about a foot long, full-bodied, with bright orange slashes beneath their jaws. Black spots thickly dotted the front portion of the body before fading along the back and then bursting forth along the tail area. They are beautiful little fish—and part of a shrinking population. They darted back to the shelter of a brushy undercut as soon as they were released.

"The North Fork is a low productivity system," said Mike Ink, formerly a fisheries biologist for the Forest Service around here. "We have to be careful of our native brood stock. It can't stand much fishing pressure. Any significant deterioration in the water quality, like, say, a failure at the Cabin Creek mine, could be devastating."

The North Fork River winds through the Kootenai Indian Trail, a centuries-old network of paths used by the tribe to travel back and forth from hunting and wintering grounds as far away as the plains east of the Continental Divide and as far west as the Pacific Ocean. The routes carried these western Indians often three times a year to their buffalo hunting grounds on the vast arid country that stretches out forever from the wild Rocky Mountain Front.

An extremely aggressive group of Blackfeet Indians eliminated an easier corridor in the southern portion of Glacier Park over Cut Bank Pass, necessitating the foraging of the far more difficult journey along the United States–Canada border. The Cut Bank crossing was not a good idea. On one occasion a clash between Siyeh (a.k.a. Mad Wolf) and his hot band of Blackfeet warriors turned into a massacre of the Kootenai, who were returning home to the coast following a successful buffalo hunt. According to the story, the Blackfeet killed, scalped, and mutilated all except an old woman.

One of the main passageways lies over and through the Kishenehn drainage that enters the North Fork near Canada. The trail climbs up through glaciated mountains, over Akima Pass, and into southeastern British Columbia. The path is part of an old Kootenai myth. Kishenehn, which means "no good," was the name given by the tribe to an adopted Piegan boy. When the youth grew up, he decided to cross the mountains and return to his own people. Several Kootenai decided to eliminate the lad. Heading toward the pass, they encountered Kishenehn along the creek. He laughed at the braves, saying that their arrows could not harm him. Unfortunately, he was wrong, and an arrow from Unknown Bear felled the unloved and unwanted individual.

My friend and I dined elegantly on corn chips, jalapeños, and more cold beer before hiking back to the truck to resume our climbing drive up the valley.

After a few bumpy miles along the road, we saw some bear grass with its tall, white, cone-shaped head, along old clearcuts that still held patches of snow next to the edges of larch and fir. The stuff looked like a large, curious, and quite silent collection of aliens transplanted from a distant lunatic galaxy. Several white-tailed deer were browsing in a meadow below, tails flicking back and forth, and an eagle was working the thermals high above a ridge. The sound of running water was everywhere, crashing along moss-covered banks, slashing through small culverts, tumbling over rock ledges, and bubbling in the creek bed. The air had cooled up here, a couple of thousand feet above the North Fork.

Another brief but steep trek brought us to a small alpine cirque lake whose surface was dimpled with the rises of hundreds of dark-bodied cutthroats, and any fly we cast in their direction brought a spirited response. Cutthroats are not known for their acrobatics and are held in low esteem by many anglers—but that's their problem. These fish went immediately to the air at the first bite of the hook and jumped a couple of times each before sounding and then coming to the net, always fighting the line in a sideways fashion. The cutts were fat, maybe two pounds, and almost black across the back. The slashes were a vibrant orange, and there were overtones of gunmetal blue along their flanks. We packed some in snow in our packs for a late dinner, sat back against a couple of trees, and lit the two big Honduran cigars I'd been saving for the occasion.

The sun worked its way farther west, more marmots whistled nearby, and a moose casually stepped out of the woods across the lake from us to stroll chest-deep into the water and dine on aquatic plants. A few small caddis flies helicoptered off the water's surface, throwing slight distortions on the mountain-cloud-sky reflection. Cigar smoke curled slowly upward and disappeared. Stillness, peace. The North Fork at its best.

We knew we eventually had to climb in the truck and drive back down the North Fork to the small town of Whitefish, where friends were expecting us for dinner, but it was tough to leave. This was one of those times when you felt like saying, "The hell with it. Let the people worry for a while. This is too good to quit." But we yielded to societal niceties, shouldering our packs and undertaking the brief hike back to our vehicle. As we crossed the divide that separated the North Fork from that of the Kootenai Forest, we paused to look back on the peaks of Glacier covered in an orange-pink sunset glow, with just a slight hint of the river glistening in an opening among the pines.

This is very fine country, and, as another friend of mine usually intones in such situations, "may it always be so."

Kootenai River

*H*undreds of trout broke the river's smooth surface as the evening feeding binge kicked into high gear on the Kootenai River. The air was warm in an early-spring way, and a light breeze casually drifted down from the forested slopes above us.

The water was flowing at 3,000 cubic feet per second, the volume controlled by the self-appointed deity known as the Army Corps of Engineers, which operates Libby Dam several miles upriver. The Kootenai once offered some of the finest wilderness fishing in North America, but the dam, dedicated by President Ford in the early seventies, inundated this pristine drainage well into Canada. Fortunately, a decent tailwater fishery of feisty rainbows has sprung up in the ensuing years.

A sizeable hatch of iron duns was providing the action this time around. A #14 pattern cast immediately to a rise form was taken aggressively by rainbows in the one- to two-pound range. Though not big by western standards, these trout are exceptionally strong—similar to Kamloops, whose genes may be mixed in here somewhere. The spirited battles always included leaps and deep runs to the rocky streambed. The same held true on a slightly diminished scale for the occasional cutthroat we encountered.

Though the current discharge was modest as far as the Kootenai flows (next to the Clark Fork it is the largest river in the state), this was still an impressive volume of water when compared to, say, the

Beaverhead in August running at 700 cfs. Sometimes the Corps really lets go and dumps 24,000 cfs. That is a lot of water roaring away toward Idaho. Even the fish seem to think so, judging from their behavior, which includes heading for the now-submerged grassy banks and at least the illusion of tranquillity.

When the rainbows move into the grasses some curious angling opportunities present themselves. The trout will begin to snatch insects (ants, beetles, grasshoppers, mayflies, caddis, or whatever happens to be crawling around) off the stems. Casting a terrestrial imitation into a field of submerged grass and then connecting with a large fish is interesting sport, if not anomalous in nature.

On this occasion, I tried an old, beat-up hopper that had fooled its share of trout in the mountain streams near home. It bounced off a stick-like stem of grass and plopped straight down in the water. A slight jerk of the line and just a touch of "upstream" mend moved the imitation a few inches. Immediately it was swallowed by a completely silver rainbow that snapped its head against the bite of the hook and the resistance of the line. Before I could get the fish on the reel, all of the slack line burned through my fingers as the trout performed its high-class, leaping rainbow number through the waving grass. It was a hell of a sight watching sixteen inches of trout dance across the water's surface and then vanish briefly behind a tall bunch of grass. The trout managed to wrap itself and the leader around some of this growth and then snap the tippet before I could release it, which was fine. I would have liked to have held the fish for just a few seconds, to have felt its heft and enjoyed the precious-metal look of its flanks.

Another hour's worth of this session produced similar results from three other rainbows that were brought boatside and then set free. A fifteen-inch rainbow weighed in around $1\frac{1}{2}$ to $1\frac{3}{4}$ pounds—a very nice fish. And the fight on a four-weight rod was spirited.

Every river has its own personality. The Kootenai's grassy banks and high water were unique in my Montana angling experiences. I wondered if much larger fish could be taken here after dark as they

Guide Dave Blackburn fishing the Kootenai below Libby Dam.

foraged among the many schools of minnows I observed frolicking in the shallows.

The river zips along at nearly six miles an hour during these periods of liquid abundance, and fishing from a drift boat is difficult. You fly past holding areas and feeding fish with such rapidity that hitting the mark is often a matter of luck, but you do get plenty of casting practice. Smaller fish are often brought to net more drowned than played out. Wading the river is folly that can quickly escalate into suicidal dimensions. Better to fish from the trusty McKenzie or stay home and wait until the river drops to a more sedate level.

Yet it is precisely the brawling nature of the Kootenai that attracts my attention here in the heart of logging country. Most of the people who live around here toil as loggers, mill workers, or miners—not exactly easy ways of making a buck. Despite being logged to virtual extinction in many places, much of the country here is still wild and tough. The peaks of the Cabinet Mountain Wilderness dominate the southwestern skyline. A few grizzlies still hang out in this backcountry.

Even at low water in the spring the river is impressive, and hatches of aquatic insects are abundant. Iron duns and blue-winged olives, along with black caddis and several species of diptera, lift off the water with predictable frequency. There is also a growing population of salmon flies that make sporadic appearances.

Consistent hatches of mayflies, including the ubiquitous *baetis,* are rarely seen until June, when the water begins to warm a bit. As summer progresses, pale evening duns and tan caddis begin to hold sway. In fact, there are times when mating swarms of the duns cloud the river's surface. I find the fishing tough because there is so much food flying around the trout that my fly is just one of millions. Angling luck must play a role in this airborne frenzy.

The fishing is best during warm, quiet evenings after seven, even stretching past eleven during the long summer nights. Taking a silvery rainbow in the last glow of the evening with the scent of pine in the air and the river swirling is good. The sides of the fish always seem to gather the last of the day's light and kick it back along the fly line. The sounds of the trout's fight mix well with those of the many birds returning to their evening roosts.

When the sun is out you will spot hundreds of whitefish holding behind rocks and in slight depressions along the streambed as you glide down the river. Most anglers hate the whitefish, but it is native to the waters of the region and provides a major source of protein for the river's rainbow population. I enjoy taking whitefish on small dries when they decide to feed on the surface. A twenty-inch whitefish is not bad action, and the fish are excellent table fare when lightly smoked. It is somewhat upsetting to see a normally conscientious fly fisher yank one out of the water, bang its head on a rock, and flip the carcass back into the trees.

Guide Dave Blackburn, who lives on the banks of the Kootenai, has taught me more about fishing here than I could have learned in a lifetime. I sometimes feel he knows some of the fish personally, but guides, of course, are also in the mythology business.

I was with Blackburn on a float in late April one year. It was calm and comfortable, and thick, dark clouds that built up in ominous ridges above the mountains rushed off over the Canadian border without doing anything to us. The river was running typically low and a little off-color—an apparent contradiction in country dominated by spring runoff until you remember the omnipresent influence of the dam. The turbidity comes from sediment delivered from logged-over tributaries in the drainage.

Even with these seemingly adverse conditions, we still managed to catch and release three dozen or so rainbows with a few cutts mixed in for variety's sake. The fish average a pound but a couple were around three, and these fought like five-pound Missouri River fish. I love the sound of a singing drag and the sight of backing ripping through the guides, and these larger trout accomplished the task with ease as they each made several long, just-below-surface runs downstream before finally being headed. Very good fish. We also hooked and lost an equal number of trout despite using our considerable angling abilities. These were smart, crafty fish. Blackburn suggested that the action had been a little on the slow side, but I could think of a hell of a lot of days when even one-tenth of it would have meant success.

"On a good day you can expect to catch more than fifty fish," said Blackburn. "I like to see the water about 3,000 cfs or even up at 5,000 cfs. Then you can pick out the holding areas better. When the water is low, the current slows down and spotting the submerged lies can be more difficult."

The word has been spreading slowly to fly fishers, but the Kootenai does not receive the smothering attention that much more famous rivers such as the Madison and Yellowstone endure. Nor is it ever likely to in the future. This part of Montana is just too far off the beaten path. Amenities such as food and a place to sleep are few and quite far between. The largest town in the area, Libby, is a logging community where you can find a good meal and a stiff drink, but you won't dine in darkened, moody surroundings with a siding salesman-turned-Tony Bennett mooning away while you chew on warmed-over, garlicky snails.

Which is as things should be here. The Kootenai is for anglers who like variety in their fishing and do not care if a certain degree of austerity is part of the package. Who needs Magic Fingers in the mattress and a dry martini when there are trout to be fished for?

The river flows for forty-eight miles below the dam-monstrosity to the Idaho border. In this stretch almost every conceivable type of habitat and fishing challenge can be found. Countless boulders, weed beds, gravel runs, bankside pocket water, and long, deep glides are solid habitat for trout as well as for insects and forage fish. Rainbows up to five pounds are caught each season, and meat fishermen take some really large guys below the dam. The fish queue up below the turbines to gorge on the churned-up fishy mess spewed forth by the power-generating turbines that suck up countless fish from the reservoir behind the dam. Some very big bull trout are found in this water as well, dining on both the bloody chum and the rainbows. Word of this sloppy banquet has also reached the eagle community. The big birds now flock here by the hundreds—like they used to on MacDonald Creek in Glacier National Park—to feast on kokanee salmon (before the population crashed in Flathead Lake after the introduction of mysis shrimp). There is also a remnant population of white sturgeon that plies its ancient way along the river's depths.

Recent regulations limiting anglers to three trout under 13 inches and one over 18 inches have led to an improvement in the quality of fishing on the river. Surveys indicate that as many as 1,300 catchable trout per mile are present in the Kootenai. I've inadvertently caught some modest-sized (five pounds) bull trout while fishing large Woolly Buggers stripped quickly from the bank back to the boat.

Starting in the high snowfields on the west slopes of the Canadian Rockies, the river flows for 485 miles through northwestern Montana and northern Idaho before swinging north up into the Kootenay Lakes of British Columbia. Next to the Yellowstone, it is the longest river in the state. The dam destroyed ninety miles (forty-eight in the United States and forty-two in Canada) of this formerly wild river. The Kootenai was once compared to the South Fork of the Flathead River in the Bob Marshall Wilderness (a couple hours to the east), one of the best cutthroat trout waters in the country.

Kokanee fishing has been good in Lake Koocanusa (the reservoir created by Libby Dam), but when the Corps draws down the water level to feed the insatiable West Coast power demands, the place looks like an ugly, muddy ditch with warm water sloshing back and forth between its banks. In the heat of August the mud cooks and stinks and then turns to filthy dust. Boat ramps and campsites are left sitting high and dry hundreds of yards from the water. At times like these, Koocanusa has all the aesthetics of a toxic waste dump. The Corps could not care less, and they told one of Montana's senators, Max Baucus, as much at a public meeting. Power comes first, weighing in with a 99 percent priority over recreation's 1 percent (in marked contrast to the pitch given to area residents when the Corps wanted to drum up public support for the project). Just another case of "Come here, boy. I'm from the government and I'm here to help you."

Blackburn points out that below the dam the fishing is as good as ever and improving some each year. There is not much in the way of serious angling pressure around here, and most of the attention comes from local enthusiasts. Roads lining both sides of the Kootenai provide relatively easy access to the water, which can be divided up into three sections.

The upper river ranges from below the Libby Dam to the town of Libby, the middle water takes in everything from town through the gorge below Kootenai Falls, and the final stretch is the miles to the Idaho border. All of this water is best covered by boat or raft, but areas such as China Rapids and the Kootenai Falls require a portage of two miles unless death by drowning is your goal. Where the Yaak River enters the Kootenai about ten miles west of Troy, some attention should be given to the standing waves that can upset your craft, especially during high water in the early part of the season.

Wading presents its own set of problems, including the strong current that is present even in periods of low water. You also need to be on the lookout for shifting water levels caused by power generation at the dam. The water can climb three or four feet in less than fifteen minutes; the change is swift but subtle. You can find yourself quickly stranded in midstream and then in serious trouble as the water continues to rise. The boys at the dam usually have a sufficient grip on reality so that a phone call placed to them prior to fishing will reveal the power generation and water release schedule.

As for the river's tributaries, the finest was, and at rare times still is, the Yaak. This narrow wilderness stream used to hold brook trout that reached twenty-four inches, but logging has devastated the drainage, especially the East Fork of the river. For the most part, the riparian corridor has been spared, so floating or wading is still a pretty experience, but the numbers of trout are way down.

One overcast day a friend and I drifted the Yaak and caught a number of brookies in the ten- to fourteen-inch range on dry flies cast to brushy holding areas. It was a lot of fun, and at times a challenge, to place a cast under overhanging growth with enough slack to obtain at least a brief drag-free float, but we never touched any brook trout of any size, and the only fish we saw over a couple of pounds were whitefish. If the river, including its headwaters, were left alone, the fishing would come back in a couple of decades. Just below Yaak Falls is a good spot to work large streamers on sink-tip lines for bull trout that are unable to move farther upstream.

There is still plenty of game around here, including moose, deer, bear, mountain lion, and grouse. Many of the small feeder creeks have healthy populations of pan-sized wild cutthroat trout that are great fun on dries fished with something like a three-weight six-foot rod.

You just dap a fly through each little run or into a bucket-sized hole and one or more little cutthroats pop up out of nowhere and take the fly. On rare occasions I've been shocked when a cutt of over a foot rises and hits my Royal Wulff. There is no room to play the fish, and I hold on while it rapidly jerks the rod tip around until it either tires or breaks off. Cutthroat of this size are always released to continue their noble, out-sized contributions to the gene pool.

These tiny Yaak and Kootenai tributaries provide some of my favorite fishing. There is an atmosphere that is both primeval and fantastically lonesome as I walk through the dark green light breathing the cool, moist cedar- and moss-scented air. The little trout have dark backs, flaming crimson slashes along their throats, and an orange-gold sheen along their lower sides—beautiful fish that taste of pine and cold water when quickly fried in a cast-iron skillet with a little butter and a squeeze of lemon juice. I could spend the rest of my life chasing trout in these streams, camping in the woods nearby, sitting around a fire, and listening to the water sparkle over the rocks.

The concentration required to make the miniature roll casts and drag-free floats is intense. I've jumped a number of black bears and one grizzly while engaged in this type of fishing. Concerning the grizzly, I first knew there was a bear around when Rupert, the family hound, collapsed to the ground and actually started moving backward. I'd never seen this method of canine locomotion before, and I was soon occupied with the sight of a clump of tag alders being rattled back and forth. Then a shiny dark brown nose and a pair of very dark eyes poked through the leaves. The grizzly at first looked like a hairy and very ugly pig. The bear walked into the water, spotted me, and stood up on its hind legs.

I thought, "Oh shit! We're dead meat," but the bear "woofed" once, dropped down to all fours, and crashed into the thick undergrowth. Back at the truck, I managed to slurp down part of a beer that sloshed from my shaking hand and dribbled down my chin and onto my shirt. Far across the stream, up on a rocky slope, I spotted the grizzly loping easily uphill and then silently over a cut in the granite ridge. No photograph would ever do justice to that adrenalin-rush, ten-second trip into the bear's world.

The Kootenai is facing threats from excessive logging, artificial flows from the Libby Dam, and heavy-metal pollution from area mines, but it is a big, strong river that will survive and eventually return to its very wild state. The Kootenai is a true northwest forest river. The sucker is too damn good to kill. The individuals who live around here and love to fish the Kootenai are probably as devoted a group of anglers as I've ever encountered. The river is in firm hands.

St. Mary River

These two huge pipes are leaking. Perhaps six feet in diameter, they are weathered black with age and rusting at the seams. Water is spouting from various holes along their length, flashing silver in the morning light. The tubes run down a gentle, grass-covered hill, across the St. Mary River, and up another hill before disappearing through aspen forest blanketing a long bluff. The liquid is being redirected, before it reaches the Canadian border, back onto Blackfeet Indian land. This has no effect on the river, though a dam some miles upstream does.

The St. Mary runs sapphire and swiftly off to the north. There are grizzlies wandering the tree-choked coulees and foraging in the meadows, digging eagerly for ground squirrels and dining on wild berries. We can't see them, but we know they are here. Tracks from coyotes, ermine, ravens, and raptors mark the damp sand between the rocks and boulders of the shoreline.

This has been a moist year, and the valley is lush and emerald under the blue of an August day. We glimpse peaks of Glacier National Park through bends in the river, their snow and ice reflecting the light in instantaneous flashes and cracklings to our eyes as the sun moves overhead. There is sound from a soft wind and the rushing water. The air smells clear and fresh with a hint of the grasses that flow easily in the breeze.

A well-established ranch lies upstream and a bridge crosses below. Wading here beneath a cut bank out of sight of anything man-made, we are alone on the Blackfeet Reservation, east of Glacier Park. This is how the land might have felt hundreds of years ago when the Blackfeet were the only people living here.

We cast our clumsy hoppers and Royal Goofus Bugs almost directly upstream, mend line furiously for a few feet of natural drift, and then watch the flies swing rapidly across the current and bounce along the uneven surface. The sun is intense, and only a few small cutthroat chase the dries. One larger fish spooks at my careless approach and zips downstream. A group of whitefish holds in a pool along the far bank, down deep, just above the many-colored gravels in the relative calm.

This is not a time to be fishing if you want to catch fish. Everything is wrong from an angling perspective: The direct light, the hot weather that hits 100 each day, the full moon, and the recent drop in water level work against us. But who cares? This is the kind of day that makes the long, deadly Montana winter survivable. It is glorious in perfection, gracing the wilderness that is the high plains, which roll in subtle waves onto the rugged shoreline of the Rocky Mountain Front. No one fishes here, though there are large cutthroat to be taken through brief and rare windows of opportunity that open just a crack when you are lucky. In periods of consistent and diminished release from Swiftcurrent Dam when there is a high overcast and hoppers are leaping blithely to their deaths on the river, or when large, dark stone flies crawl out from the water to dry on warm rocks and then take flight in the pure sky above, trout can be fooled. How often does this happen? I don't know. Maybe only a few days each year.

This time my friend and I do not experience the kind of fishing that would grow into pedestrian hyperbole over the brutal months of cold that never seem very far away. Today's memories take a different form. Sensations of light, comfortable air, cold water, and intense green define our experience on the St. Mary. (And those ancient, rotting pipes singing with kinetic energy. When and where will they explode? Perhaps alongside the decaying steel girder bridge where we parked?)

Besides, this curious river with its obvious delights is also a marvelous excuse to buzz (and if you travel with my friend, "buzz" is the proper word as we hit seventy near Logan Pass on one narrow, empty stretch) over the Going-to-the-Sun Road at dawn from Whitefish, before the crowds of visitors wake up and hit the bricks in search of wildlife and vertigo. It's a chance to spend several or more hours casting nymphs and streamers in a couple of the many lakes, ponds, and reservoirs that have very big trout lurking in them. The following description is a representative (and mostly truthful) example of the fishing in these still waters.

We were the only people fishing a certain Blackfeet Reservation lake. The crest of the Rocky Mountain Front was visible in the west, and the day's first light was shading softly from pink to salmon and on through red-orange along the summit. On just the third cast of the first morning a huge fish was on, right next to shore in the shallows and reed beds. Then, one jump out of the smooth water by a rainbow far more intent on freedom than on giving a transitory display of acrobatic ability. My friend was straining well back against the vertical plane trying to stop the trout as it torpedoed among the remains of last year's thick reed beds. The powerful graphite eight-weight rod put on a well-flexed show of strength with marginal results in the early going. A dozen minutes of this submarine behavior from the trout, and the fight was over. Thumb and forefinger would not reach around the narrowest portion of the tail of the fish, which was in bright spawning color with a humped back and well-defined kype. This was a big trout—long past five pounds.

This first fish proved to be the biggest, but there were a few others from two pounds up to maybe seven, with many of greater heft spotted cruising the shallows during two perfect spring days of "ice-out" fishing on the reservation.

A cutthroat taken from the Blackfeet Reservation lake.

Not all that many anglers fish here during the halcyon days of summer, and the place is borderline empty in April and May when the big trout move up from the deep water and begin their spawning ritual on the shallow-water gravel shelves in many of the forty-plus lakes and ponds that contain healthy numbers of large fish. This is the one time of the year when a person who works hard for a week has an honest chance at a ten-pound trout. And they can be present anytime of the day—morning, noon, or late afternoon (tribal regulations prohibit angling after sunset). Yet, aside from tribal members, the only people we saw fishing here lived in Montana, and they numbered less than a dozen on the four lakes we worked during our brief foray.

The fishing here is hard work. It is for the serious angler only. Anyone expecting a casual Montana blue-ribbon stream experience is in for a big surprise, and possibly an unpleasant one at that.

The plan is to get here just as the ice is leaving a lake or has been gone at the most one week. This is prime time for big-time action, when a well-placed pattern worked right in front of the trout often provokes a serious response.

Even though the fish are "spawning," you are not endangering the future of the rainbow population. The lakes of the reservation do not provide sufficient water movement, cover, or depth in the gravel areas to ensure successful reproduction. These populations are the result of an ongoing planting program that is monitored each year by the tribe. Once on the loose, the trout quickly turn spooky and selective in the lakes, but they are not self-sustaining.

Depending on the ferocity of the mostly spent winter, the lakes on the Blackfeet reservation begin to open up in late March and continue the process for about eight weeks. When a given body of water is open or at its peak depends in large part on elevation and size and whether it is fed by springs. Inlets and outlets in these high plains lakes have, at most, a very small influence on the scheme of things.

To fish here at this time of year, you have to be willing to accept crazy swings in the conditions from heat and wind to rain and wind to snow and wind (but always the wind). You really need to bring clothing for four seasons. Our April visit was in the mid-seventies, but one week later the temperature nose-dived into the twenties, and rough air racing down off the Rocky Mountain Front made fishing impossible.

Most of the reservation's 1.8 million acres stretch out on seemingly desolate high plains country, with a few lakes up in the timbered foothills of the mountains. Elk, deer, and grizzlies wander all of this country. The northern part of the territory can be "woolly," according to Blackfeet guide Joe Kipp of Browning. What Joe is saying is that some of the isolated streams flowing in from Glacier Park, especially the ones that look so inviting to anglers, are world-class grizzly habitat. Joe grew up here and refuses to fish most of them, especially the brushy stretches that mask an angler's presence. Walk into a griz here and you lose the game: nowhere to run, nowhere to hide.

What attracts the attention of Joe and a small but dedicated number of fly fishers is the chance to connect with a big trout. Growth rates in these fertile waters are hard to believe. According to the U.S. Fish and Wildlife Service, trout can grow from eight to eleven inches a year, and a two-year-old rainbow will approach two feet and six pounds in the bigger waters. Joe backs up this information by noting that trout average "an inch a month for twenty-four months."

How big the fish really do grow is an unanswered question, but a five-pound trout does not overly excite anyone who has fished the area more than once. I know that my scale of reference jumps up a notch when I make the eastward drive over Marias Pass on U.S. Highway 2 from my home in Whitefish.

So if the fishing is so damn good, why isn't the place overrun with anglers flinging every angling contraption known to man at anything that swims? There are several good reasons. The first and probably the meanest is the wind. Conservatively, one day in four will be rendered unfishable because of the breezes that can blow steadily at over 30 miles an hour and gust up to levels that knock you over. Joe tells of car windows being blown out, and points out several mobile homes that were obliterated by a 100-mile-per-hour blast last year.

Even on calm days in the 20-mile-per-hour range the fishing is tough. The wind usually comes out of the southwest, so you want to work the northeast shores because the constant wave action scours the spawning gravels clean, attracting the trout. Unfortunately, you are casting into the teeth of the gale when wading, and when working from a float tube you expend an awful lot of energy trying to stay in casting position.

The second reason, to be honest, is that there are plenty of times when you can work long hours without turning up many fish. The reservation is a very off-and-on situation.

Casting spinning gear is a bit easier than working a flyrod, but it is not recommended. Snagging fish is now illegal, and using spinning gear will inadvertently lead to "snagged" fish. The tribe is responding to complaints from upset fly fishers and is gradually shifting its emphasis to fly fishing. You do not want to try to explain yourself to a tribal warden, who is looking for people winging big spoons with the hooks flared out into the water and jerked back, with stocking the larder their only goal.

Another problem is finding both the lakes and the fish. Tribal regulations have what appears to be a good map on the reverse side, but signs marking roads into lakes such as Hidden (believe me, it is well named) are either difficult to spot or nonexistent. And if the rains come you will be stuck in gumbo mud. Two-lane trails pass for roads here, and they can turn into axle-deep quagmires in a hurry. Local ranchers make a lot of money towing people back to the highway with their four-wheel-drive tractors whenever a freak spring snowstorm hits and then quickly melts away in the next day's hot sun.

As mentioned earlier, the reservation is not a wild trout fishery. Up until about 1980 most of these waters were barren. Chance plantings of an experimental nature revealed the fecundity of the water and spawned this fertile angling.

A lake that is great one year, however, can be frozen out or past its prime or even poisoned out by tribal managers the next year. You just don't know. Checking at sporting goods stores in towns like Browning, East Glacier, and Cut Bank will get you pointed in the right direction. Talking with other anglers helps fine-tune the process. (Most of them should be helpful if they've spent any time dealing with the frustrations here.) And if you have the money, hiring a guide for a couple of days will ease you into the routine and help you get a feel for the land. Some of the best water is on private land, and the only way to gain access is with the help of a Blackfeet tribal member. Getting to some lakes involves opening and closing barbed-wire gates and navigating a confusing network of dirt "roads." There is just no sure thing. Check out the situation before you leave home and when you hit Browning. There are always plenty of lakes with fish in them, but it is a fluctuating situation.

Finally, the only place to stay on the reservation is in Browning, and this is not the place to go looking for nightlife if you are not a tribal member. Get a room and check in. Keep an eye on your gear. Go eat and then have a drink or two in the room. Night life moves at its own pace around here and, even among tribal members, that drink or two has been known to escalate into violence. Non-tribal visitors can inadvertently trigger latent anger toward the "outside world." That's just the way things are on the reservation. When we fished with Joe, who is a tribal member, he kept reminding us to lock our rigs and bring our valuables along on the day's fishing. As a result, we had no problems.

An example of why there exists a certain amount of resentment toward non-Blackfeet around here concerns some well-meaning fly fishers west of the mountains. These guys were justifiably appalled by the sight of Indians driving along the shorelines of the lakes looking for spawning trout. When the fish were spotted, the car stopped and a treble hook was cast out over them, they were snagged, and thrown into a cooler. This is an ugly sight and a bad situation; tribal authorities have made the practice illegal and are embarked on a slow but successful education process aimed at eliminating snagging.

According to a tribal member I spoke with, the fly fishers collected a fairly healthy sum of money, which they entrusted to one of their group, who was the appointed envoy to the Blackfeet Nation. The intent was to give the tribe the cash to hire a warden to police the area and stop the snagging. Instead, the effort managed to create further anger in the Blackfeet toward the white race.

One suspects, after speaking with a number of tribal members, that it would not take too many incidents like this one to lead the council to seriously consider closing fishing to the outside world. These people are not dependent on money from anglers, and cutting off the fishing would not be a major hardship.

With all of this mayhem and confusion, you may wonder: Why bother in the first place? Simple. Because there is the chance that you'll hit one of those days when the fish are present in good numbers and the weather is somewhat cooperative and you will catch big trout—maybe lots of strong, big rainbows that will tear into your backing in nothing flat.

One good thing about the nearly constant wind is that it almost always blows out of the southwest, which sometimes simplifies finding the fish. During ice-out, always work the northeast shores along the exposed gravel bars. If this fails, wade out or use a float tube and fish along the edge of shallow and deep water with an intermediate line, gently retrieving a small scud or even a large nymph in olive or brown. A Prince or a Sheep Creek always takes good fish. Try to locate lines of submerged weed beds and work your pattern either down between them or just above them. Finally, try working between and right up to last year's reed beds, where the trout love to hide.

A lesson I've learned fishing here the past couple of seasons is that by late July much of the best water is choked with weeds and the trout have gone way down deep to sulk and ponder their fate out in the "big open." You will see few if any fish working during the day, and swimming a nymph through this dense growth is damn near impossible. In water such as this, any trout you take will be a propitious collision with good fortune. Come evening, the monsters drift up to take small mayflies. The swirls they make are awe inspiring. Prime time is always well after sunset, a cruel fate but an incredible sight to behold. Trophy trout voodoo in the gathering gloom with maybe the sound of a coyote wailing at the rising moon from a far ridge or a nighthawk working just overhead with the thin outline of those massive mountains running away in the west. You don't need to take these fish. Knowing they exist is sufficient.

One day I took photographs of two groups of anglers working separate pods of trout along a 200-yard stretch of gravel bar. The fish were circling and swirling over the gravel, often porpoising out over the crest of a wave. Every few minutes or so one of the anglers would get his streamer or large nymph right in front of a fish with a short, striping retrieve. Frequently the trout would nail the thing and head out for deep water. The struggle tended to run well below in the rough water and would last several minutes. The fish never spooked and the action remained constant for a couple of hours. Then the trout dived back to the depths.

Or there was the late afternoon we fished a lake with the peaks of Glacier glowing as the sun dropped slowly behind them. The ice was just twenty feet from shore and making a hushed tinkling sound as it pushed against itself in the evening breeze. Small pockets of open water no bigger than the bed of a pickup revealed large rainbows cruising back and forth beneath the ice. You had to cast your fly to these "pools," letting your line rest on the ice and hope that when a fish did take, your leader didn't shear on the sharp frozen surfaces. There were two ways to approach the situation: wear neoprene chest waders and stalk the fish from shore or wear the same waders, climb into a float tube, and quietly paddle up to the ice and make a short, delicate cast from water level. Both methods produced. More trout escaped than were landed, but it was truly exciting angling in a wild, beautiful setting.

Later in the summer Joe invited me over for a day of fishing some of the small streams that pour out of the Rocky Mountains. One July morning we headed off into the hills, crossing through many barbed-wire gates that we made sure were closed after our passing.

The dirt road quickly diminished into a series of ruts that wound up and down rocky hills, across muddy depressions, and through thick stands of aspen and willow in the creek bottoms. Rain squalls sailed by overhead, sometimes throwing hail. After an hour or so we were far away from the Blackfeet Highway that runs from the Canadian border into Browning. Brightly colored mountains in orange, blue-gray, ochre, and buff thrust out onto the plains. These are the advance guard of the overthrust belt, a vast and complex geologic formation that runs along the northern Rocky Mountain Front. A small creek bubbled over a rock bed, occasionally cutting into earthen banks, running under dead falls, and breaking out into minute braided channels that raced over gravel bars.

In the fall, large bull trout move up here to spawn. The spectacle of five-pound, maybe ten-pound, fish lit up in breeding colors like a psychotic sunset, wriggling through inches of water in the middle of this beautiful nowhere, was something I had to see. Small cutthroat live here year-round, and that is what we were after. I noticed Joe strapping on a .44 magnum pistol loaded with hollow points.

"Don't worry, John," he laughed. "I'll make sure any grizzlies get you long before I have to use this. We have to get even somehow."

I was encouraged. There I was, fishing with a Blackfeet Indian miles from anywhere on his home turf, and he was talking about "evening the score." I was quickly caught up in the rhythms of this mountain-stream angling that produced some little, wild fish who tugged and splashed against the force of the flyrod. It was fun fishing made special by Joe's willingness to share an experience that is normally off limits to non-tribal members.

"Some of our religious places are around here, a little farther up the stream, places you call 'vision-quest sites,'" said Joe. "There is a spot that is haunted by one of our members who lived hundreds of years ago. Today if any of us go up to that mountain to sleep and have 'visions,' the spirit yells and tells us to go away because we stink from what we eat. Our diet has much modern food in it and this smells bad to the spirit. If we try and spend the night here, he throws us off the mountain.

"I know that for you to believe this is difficult or maybe not possible, but for us, this is our way of life, physically and spiritually. We draw our strength from this belief in our history and spirits.

"The boundaries of Glacier Park mean nothing to us. They are things of your culture. The boundaries we recognize are those drawn by the mountains, the plains over there," and Joe's hand swept across the northeastern horizon, off into the distance that is Alberta. "Where a creek runs defines the land for us or where the elk gather on the plains during a certain time of the year. And, of course, where the grizzlies are."

Joe laughed, patted the pistol, and told me to walk ahead of him. He'd keep an eye on the trail behind us and also make sure he kept the truck in view. This did seem like a hell of an idea.

We spent the rest of the day exploring waters like this small creek. And we caught silvery cutthroat in deep pools of cool blue that tumbled over flat rocks before racing on along coarse, red gravels. Massive mountain walls displayed petroglyphs drawn by Joe's ancestors centuries ago. They were painted on rock faces hundreds of feet from the valley floor with a mixture of animal blood and fat.

"Some scientists have tried to improve on our paint, but they can't. Our people used to swing out over those cliffs on ropes to do the painting," said Joe, and I thought that there was no way in hell you'd get me over the edge up there.

Joe told me stories of the trips young members of the tribe made to Mexico to hunt jaguar for their pelts, which were used in ceremonies back home. Or other journeys above the arctic to take polar bear for the same purpose. These people took life seriously, if an investment of three years of one's life in pursuit of ceremony is any indication, and that is how long these quests took.

I can see this taking place on "Leave It To Beaver." Ward staggers through the door after work and asks, "June, honey, where are the kids?"

June swishes in wearing high heels and a cocktail dress, exhausted from a rough day of staring out the window over the kitchen sink, and explains, "Wally and the Beaver took Lumpy's car down to Oaxaca to hunt a few jaguars. You know the boys. Something about needing something for their club house."

"What?" Ward storms after June, who is off to the kitchen again in search of antique China coffee cups.

We worked some more water that would never be the inspiration for big-fish dreams, but it didn't matter. These creeks were wild and beautiful and held native trout that were rarely fished over. Perhaps they are the last members of a dying breed.

I asked Joe about the St. Mary, and he said that there are some big fish in the river, but they are extremely hard to catch. They are spooky, and the dam discharges screw up the fishing most of the time.

"You're going to keep fishing there until you take a big cutthroat, aren't you, John?" I smiled and so did Joe. Shared addictions.

After some days of this type of adventure, I understood the growing attraction, the internal pulling I feel whenever I think of the Blackfeet Reservation. The chance to catch huge rainbows (and, in some cases, brooks and cutts and other species) is an opportunity not to be passed over. It is a rare privilege, one to be valued and respected. The fishing is special and, at times, very good, but it is only a small part of the appeal. There are also the small streams, the wide-open plains stretching off to infinity, the grizzlies, the Rocky Mountain Front, and people like Joe with a family-tribal history far older than mine—all of the fantastic, natural magic that sizzles out in the honest open.

I know I'll never get enough of this country.

Bitterroot River

The river had changed drastically since last spring when I had spent a quiet afternoon roaming its banks with an angling friend. We weren't fishing, just chasing a winter's worth of cabin fever by walking and pointing out rising fish to each other.

Today was only a few months after that April day, when the drought-plagued summer of 1988 did not seem possible. That summer, rivers, lakes, and reservoirs throughout Montana suffered through parched times. Many turned bone dry, and the trout went belly up. Fires ravaged Yellowstone National Park, and smoke filled the air as far away as the Pacific Ocean. Everyone was mad at someone—the public at the Park Service for "allowing" the park to go up in flames, smoke, and ashes; anglers at ranchers for sucking the rivers dry to water their crops; and ranchers at anglers for pointing this fact out to anyone who would listen. In many streams and lakes the trout still have not fully recovered, but they will, given a little time.

On this visit in late August, mayflies and caddis flies rose around me in abundance and rainbows and browns of healthy proportions rose eagerly to take them, but the river's flow was diminished so much that it resembled a large creek more than a strong western river. Most of the snow in the rugged Bitterroot Range to the west and the lower Sapphires to the east had long since melted.

This is the Bitterroot River, one of the best fly fishing streams in Montana. Even in its current desiccated state, the trout fishing holds its own. The growth rate for its fish is half again that of its more-famous counterpart nearby, Rock Creek.

Although many fish had moved out of the river and back into small spring creeks in order to survive this year's severe drought, a number of trout still held in deep pools, in quiet backwaters, under logjams, and in swirling eddies.

In fact, like in many other rivers in the state, the fish were concentrated in the dwindling number of good holding areas and were being hammered by the fly fisherman's burden, "meat" fishermen. Montana's game wardens had their hands full this season. All the same, the fishing was fun, full of action and challenge. The challenge came from trying to place a dry fly directly in a feeding lane of a trout, now turned highly spooky and selective because of the low water level.

Browns to fifteen inches and rainbows averaging a little bigger provided the acrobatic sport. For years I had labored under the mistaken belief that brown trout were not jumpers, but the last few years had proved me wrong. From the Beaverhead to the Madison to here in the Bitterroot valley of southwestern Montana, brown trout of every shape and size displayed a remarkable proclivity for airborne resistance.

In just a few hours of wading and casting along a section of the river about twenty-five miles south of Missoula, I had netted about two dozen fish, the largest eighteen inches and the average better than twelve. It was enjoyable fishing in the warm temperatures of summer. A light, dry zephyr made the low-nineties level comfortable.

The fishing seemed a little strange in the smoky air that obscured the mountains guarding the valley. Fire, though many miles away, could spread with the speed of interstate traffic in this wind, heat, and dryness. (A few weeks later, in September, a crown fire racing through the tops of a dense stand of lodgepole pine along the western edge of Glacier National Park ripped through some sections of trees at nearly sixty miles an hour. The conflagration, triggered by the discarded cigarette from a careless logger in the Red Meadow Creek drainage, claimed the life of a firefighter.)

Things had been very dry for the latter part of the eighties, so this was not the first time I'd caught trout with the smell of burning forests in the winds. A couple of years earlier, clouds of the stuff had drifted hundreds of miles down from the wildfires scorching the wilderness prairies of British Columbia and Alberta. Several weeks of breathing this smoke, and my lungs were raw and my eyes constantly tearing and bloodshot. Fire and smoke were becoming a pain-in-the-ass fact of late-summer life in the northwest.

But back to the Bitterroot, which is formed when the east and west forks join forces near Connor. The river flows for approximately seventy miles from this point, with a drop in elevation of only around 800 feet before flowing into the Clark Fork near Fort Missoula.

Rainbows, browns, brookies, cutthroats, bull trout, assorted hybrids, and, unfortunately, northern pike are found in the river, along with numerous smaller forage fish, whitefish, and suckers. The trout purist in me says "unfortunately" regarding the northern pike invasion, but the last few years, especially in late spring, have seen some outrageous pike fishing with large streamers, barracuda patterns, tarpon patterns, fabric remnants lashed to grappling hooks, and just about anything else that can approximate life in the water. Shock tippets are necessary to offset the razor-like effects of the thousands of teeth lining the pikes' mouths. Hefty rods to turn the fish, which swoop up out of nowhere to hammer your pattern, are also a good idea. Although the pike provide excellent sport, the influx of these interlopers has caused some problems among the salmonids. Pike, especially the twenty-pound boys, eat a lot of fish.

The trout can also reach truly impressive sizes, even in the small feeder creeks and in the irrigation ditches and canals that parallel the river for a good deal of its length. Fish exceeding ten pounds have been recorded but are extremely rare and are probably more a result of being in the right place at the right time than of angling expertise.

On an extended visit to the region, some time should be devoted to fishing one or more of the creeks in the drainage, which frequently contain good numbers of healthy rainbows, cutthroats, brooks, and browns in relatively pristine settings.

I remember one late-summer day when I followed a two-lane "road" along a diminutive flow leading through open rangeland that gave way to thick forest in the Sapphires. Once above the irrigated fields, whose needs decimated the stream flow, I came upon a section of creek that offered pool after turquoise pool, each loaded with colorful, feisty rainbows and cutts that came readily to a dry fly. I caught dozens of fish ranging from six to twelve inches in a quarter-mile section.

Wading wet and working a Royal Wulff through each riffle, run, and bubbling pool was a riot. The fish were unsophisticated, leaping and splashing as they chased the fly, often in twos and threes. You could catch a hundred fish in an afternoon and I did, on several occasions, working my way a quarter of a mile or so downstream with one fly and back up again with another, knowing all the while that a beer or two were waiting for me ice-cold in a brisk riffle next to a shaded bank.

A good deal of this land is on national forest, which provides easy access. The streams on the east side have more nutrients and, as a result, are more productive. The drainages on the west side are in the process of being logged to death. If you'd like to fish them and do not believe in reincarnation, I suggest that you make the effort in the next few years. Trees grow back very slowly here, and streambeds take a couple of decades or so to return to normal after being clogged with sediment from the construction of logging roads.

The Bitterroot is accessible its entire length by a number of bridges crossing the river and on various parcels of public land. Inquiries locally will reveal their locations. Permission is still generally given to those who take the time to ask property owners for access through their holdings. Perhaps the best way to fish the river is to float a medium-length section of six or seven miles, stopping along the numerous gravel bars to get out and wade. Throughout much of the season the fish lie close to the banks and casts need to be banged right to the edge and then mended upstream. Humpies, Wulffs, and stone fly imitations in season all work well.

Once the runoff begins, forget about fishing the main river. Millions of tons of snowmelt pour out of the mountains and wash through the valley. Things often don't return to normal until July. Side channels and the mouths of feeder streams are the best locations during runoff.

As the water warms up during the summer, riffles become more productive, especially during late morning through afternoon. I've rarely fished the Bitterroot, or any other river for that matter, at the crack of dawn. True, the fishing is often great, but rising that early reminds me too much of work, so I pass up the possible increase in action for the sake of my own dearly cherished laziness and comfort.

The Bitterroot has often yielded excellent catches from early afternoon through the heat of the day, with the fish holding in sun-sheltered locations. Muddler minnows worked next to shore and stripped back to the raft also provide action at these "off" times.

Back in my college days when I did not have the money to rent a boat or access to borrow one, I often drove along the back roads along the east side of the river and pulled over at a promising spot. Cutoffs, tennis shoes, and a T-shirt was the preferred outfit during this summertime pursuit. A box of flies, tipped material, pocket knife, floatant, and waterproofed fishing license was the only tackle taken along in addition to rod and reel.

The Bitterroot was warm enough to eliminate any chance for a hypothermic disaster, and I would wade out into the flow, bouncing and bobbing downstream, casting a hopper pattern almost at water level to likely-looking areas. Playing a decent-sized trout while drifting chest deep or more downriver was a unique and exciting way to fish. Admittedly, there were some dangers attendant with this method, like drowning or being run over by a raft, but what the hell, it was still worth the risk.

Stone flies begin showing up in April and are generally around most of the season. Caddis flies also put in an appearance in late April and hatch throughout the rest of the year, along with mayflies, which punch in with a degree of consistency in midsummer. The legendary salmon fly hatch can begin as early as mid-May, but it usually peaks a couple of weeks later.

An early spring hatch of the little-known Skwala stone fly is one of the best times to connect with browns in the twenty-inch and up range. Few anglers are aware of this action, so you have the water pretty much to yourself. The insects become active around the second week in March and last into the first ten days of April, tapering off as the runoff from the spring snowmelt begins in earnest.

"On a warm day you can take browns that run up to twenty-seven inches," says John Adza of Catch Montana. He describes the Skwala as a flat-shaped creature, dark olive and size 6–8, and adds that he has never seen them take to the air despite being winged. This spring was the first time I'd ever fished the hatch and even though the weather was wet, I lucked out and found the insects and caught some nice browns that did not behave in a particularly discriminating fashion.

Skwalas' hatching, which differentiates them from their famous salmon fly relatives, is not marked by wild, blizzard-like extravaganzas that move steadily upriver day by day. Instead, the Skwala exhibits a more sedate behavior, hatching on a localized basis (which means I was fortunate to find the buggers on my own) throughout the stream course in pretty much the same spots year after year. Once you turn up a spot or two, you can return each spring and, with a little searching, tie into some good big brown action.

After the runoff, when the river has settled down some, caddis patterns come into their own, and when fishing in the afternoon and evening I stick exclusively with dries. I probably catch fewer fish than those who probe the depths, but I'm not all that aggressive and I like the sight of an Elk Hair Caddis bouncing along the surface of the clear water that shimmers gold and copper from the streambed gravels.

A rainbow taken during the Bitterroot Skwala hatch in March.

And when a nice trout dashes up to hit the fly, the sight of the take is as much fun as the fight itself. This pattern and the Royal Wulff in #10–14 are all I bring with me on these balmy outings. I usually catch fish. When I don't, so what? The river and valley are fantastic and the casting is always entertaining.

From August through September, attractor patterns like the Royal Wulff and some of the more garishly colored Humpies and Irresistibles attract the attention of better trout everywhere, especially in the riffles and eddies.

A good selection of the previously mentioned dries in sizes #10–16 will be adequate, along with hoppers in sizes #8–12. Muddlers in sizes #8–10 are appropriate. I've also had some success with sculpin, Spruce, Zonker, and Woolly Bugger patterns in the #2–4 range, but these have always seemed like work to fish properly and the Bitterroot is, to my way of thinking, primarily a dry-fly piece of water.

In the fall the browns are on the move to their spawning grounds or already over their redds. The fish will be fewer in number most of the time during these months, but they run larger. This is one time I prefer streamers. I look for newly scoured channels in the gravel, places that big browns definitely prefer. Cleaner gravels and less sediment equal more oxygen to the eggs and a higher percentage of fry emergence.

When the sun is out this time of year, work the banks beneath tall cottonwood trees, now turning bright yellow with the cooling of the nights. Browns abandon their redds in favor of bank security.

The best Woolly Bugger angler I know is Tom Rosenbauer, who works for Orvis in Vermont. Watching the guy zip a Bugger tight to the bank, make three quick, six-inch strips, and then cast again, all the time working quickly downstream, is an education. When the fish are present he'll take one on about every third cast. As he says, if a fish doesn't hit in the first three strips, don't waste your time. Pick up the line and cast again a few feet downstream. He calls this sport "buggering the banks," and it produces extremely well.

When floating I prefer an 8'6'' rod that handles as light as a weight-

forward-four line and a nine-foot leader tapering to 3X or 4X. Many
of the valley's guides who know the river better than I do use heav-
ier equipment, up to seven-weight and 2X tippets. The lighter setup
appeals to me because it offers more action, is more responsive, and
is less tiring to use during a long day on the water. If this costs me a
big fish, those are the breaks. I can live with the loss.

When wading, I like a rod that is a little longer, maybe 9'0", and
one that can handle a six-weight line. This gives me a little more casting length, which offsets some of the ability I would have to have to
get close to a good lie when fishing from a raft.

One of the true advantages to fishing the Bitterroot is the fact that
food, accommodations, fishing gear, and just about everything else
are readily available and easy to find. U.S. Highway 93 travels the entire length of the river. Starting in the north with Missoula and working south, towns such as Florence, Stevensville, Victor, Corvallis,
Hamilton, and Darby all offer adequate facilities for the fisherman.

A decidedly interesting, change-of-pace way to check out the river
is afforded by the Teller Wildlife Refuge, which offers an angling experience of a slightly different nature. Located just outside of Corvallis approximately forty-five miles south of Missoula, the refuge totals
1,300 acres at present, but is growing each year with new acquisitions
being made as property becomes available for sale in the area. The
refuge is part of a growing trend in the West that gains its impetus
from private conservationists. Teller was founded a few years back by
Otto Teller, a Californian in his eighties who is committed to fish,
wildlife, and land conservation.

There are numerous small streams and spring creeks on the property, plus a sizeable portion of frontage along the Bitterroot River. As
with the main river, the refuge's streams abound with rainbow,
brown, brook, and cutthroat trout. Any type of fishing that can be
found elsewhere in the valley can also be found here and in relative
privacy in scenic surroundings that refuge manager Chris Miller is
working aggressively to restore to a natural state.

A number of streams flow through tall-grass meadows and offer a true, hunting-smart-fish challenge for the skilled fisherman. "In this type of water, you stalk the trout and once you find one, you try and make a perfect cast to where he is holding," said Miller.

Over 200 species of wildlife pass through or make the refuge their permanent home. These include great horned owls, pileated woodpeckers, white-tailed deer, ducks, pheasants, geese, beaver, blue herons, and osprey. Elk are also occasionally spotted.

The refuge is open to a small number of individuals each year. The groups are usually limited to four adult friends or family members who stay in a restored 1880s homestead. Teller is a finely tuned, civilized, and relaxed way to fish in the Bitterroot.

This casual nature of the Bitterroot is a very pleasant change of pace from some of the hectic and increasingly uncomfortable fishing found today on rivers like the Bighorn and the Madison. These rivers and some others in the West are being loved to death and are now undergoing ugly growing pains. Anglers swear at each other. Some toss rocks in the water near where others are fishing. Fistfights break out on exceptionally crowded, and usually hot, days. Perhaps a permit system is needed to restore order and dignity to the rivers.

So far the Bitterroot has weathered all challenges. I don't think it will ever produce as many really large trout as either the Madison or the Bighorn—which will keep the thundering herd of big-fish fanatics down to a mostly dedicated crew of serious fly fishers who enjoy the finer things in angling life. For those of us who like our trout and our rivers in beautiful, serene surroundings, this river is hard to beat.

Rock Creek

$\mathcal{S}$ tanding in the middle of Rock Creek, I thought I had been transported to a surreal landscape filled with small, flapping wings and thousands of strips of bright orange swarming in the soft air. The pine-covered slopes looked down on a scene of complete chaos. The annual salmon fly extravaganza was in full swing. Trout everywhere were making grand, leaping appearances as they indulged in this luscious insect banquet put on for them by those kind souls at Mother Nature & Company.

Brown trout, rainbow trout, cutthroat trout, brook trout, occasionally an ebullient bull trout—all were jumping to the salmon fly rag. Truly, this was an example of salmonid overindulgence.

A Sofa Pillow plopped on the water was swallowed in a flurry of piscatorial gluttony. It was a western Montana orgy for fish and angler alike, one that has been raging on this free-flowing stream from late spring through early summer for eons.

I gave up and waded to shore. The frenzy of activity was too much. The whirring of the salmon flies and the slashing rises of the trout were a heady combination. I walked back to the truck, wondering how far upstream the bash would have wandered by tomorrow.

That was the shape of things on the stream some years ago when the timing was perfect and the fishing was superb. Proper planning and skill had nothing to do with success. Hitting the right part of the water just in front of this wave of *Pteronarcys californica* was all that was required. The first Sofa Pillow offered to the trout ricocheted off two of the bulky, lumbering creatures on its turbulent way over the creek, reminiscent of the passing of the famous Scooter Line of the Chicago Blackhawks in the sixties. A couple of crisp passes across the ice (or, in today's case, through the pure air), a slapshot (a soft landing on the water) toward a crouching goalie (feeding trout), and the puck was in the net (Fish on!).

When this barrage of activity is in full swing on the water almost every trout around is vulnerable to an artificial that is bushy and large. This is literally a freshwater form of a shark feeding frenzy. Mature and supposedly wise fish lose all trace of caution as they race about pools and deep glides in hot pursuit of the airborne concentrations of protein. Bulky stone fly nymphs, dragged up toward the surface in a Leisenring Lift in an imitation of the difficult voyage to the freedom of the open air, drive the trout nuts. Sometimes they gorge to the extent that coaxing them up to the surface to take a dry fly is next to impossible for weeks after the hatch. The trout are stuffed.

Things are not always so easy on Rock Creek, but the few times everything has clicked during the salmon fly hatch are sufficient to justify the place's revered status with legions of fly fishers. For the expert this is a spot to take trout that are crafty and experienced in the devious behavior practiced by anglers. These big fish are not easy marks. For the novice there are decent numbers of "dumb" cutthroat, rainbow, brook, and even brown trout to cast over with a fair chance of hooking up with a couple during the day.

Rock Creek's worldwide reputation caused serious problems in the seventies, but the stream is resilient, and with the implementation of special regulations the fishing is slowly improving. Prior to 1980 not many rainbows over sixteen inches were showing up, and browns of twenty inches were a definite rarity. State fisheries biologists and anglers were alarmed. This downturn in the level of angling at Rock

Rock Creek in early September.

Creek (and other streams throughout the state) was partially the result of Montana's nationwide publicity about the state's "blue ribbon" streams during the seventies. These waters were usually described as some of the best in the world, so if you were an out-of-state angler, where would you go? The effect was immediate and devastating. In 1979 Rock Creek became one of the first areas to institute artificial lures only, unless you were under 15 years old. The current limit is three fish per day under twelve inches or two under twelve and one over twenty.

According to Missoula resident Tony Acerrano, fishing editor for *Sports Afield,* the fishing has not yet returned to the excellence of the early seventies, but the numbers and size of the trout, especially the rainbows, is slowly and steadily improving. Although he prefers to fish dries on this stream, he admits to consistently taking rainbows with a Prince drifted through the riffles and faster runs. Acerrano adds that he is a substantially better angler than he was way back when, yet the size of the trout he is taking now is smaller, an indication that things can still stand some improvement.

Early in the season, through June, waders should look out for rafts operated by several outfitters permitted by the U.S. Forest Service. The narrowness of much of the stream makes for tricky navigating at times and has triggered some spirited controversy lately.

Rock Creek does travel through some wild country, but wading this water is not an isolated, wild adventure. Even on weekdays you will encounter yupsters driving BMWs, Mercedes, and Jaguars with California license plates (or New York or Illinois, for that matter) clad in forty thousand bucks of the latest, top-of-the-line gear. Some of these guys even know how to fish.

As a result, in addition to being a quality fishery, Rock Creek is one of the planet's prime people-watching locations. Spending an entire morning observing neoprene-clad individuals wandering thigh-deep in the water, studiously bowed as they observe the antics of various species of aquatic fauna is fun and enlightening. You'll see them deftly and stealthily work their way closer, ever closer toward a spent caddis, mayfly, or less-than-alert stone fly. Some of them have those special glasses with the little magnifying sections built in. And they come armed with nets and small bottles filled with killing compounds to store the specimens in. When I was much younger, capturing bees in an old peanut butter jar was considered a worthwhile pursuit, but judging from the frenetic attention directed toward these insects, the obvious conclusion is that my youth was misspent. This behavior may go on for more than an hour before the fly fisher is suitably prepared to actually cast a pattern with any degree of seriousness. The only hitch to this observational dance is that nine times out of ten people will proceed to work the exact same water they just finished tromping through. Even derelict writers know better than to engage in this futility. No *Salmo trutta* (forgive me, I get carried away every now and then) in his or her right mind would still be finning around a run that just had the human equivalent of a D-9 cat marauding through it. Fish have small brain pans, but their survival instincts are finely honed. All of that eye strain is for nothing. I'd rather spook the *Salmo gairdneri* (or is the proper term *oncorhynchus* now?) with my leader as it drags a Bucktail Caddis under the surface. At least my illusion of having a realistic chance to catch a fish remains intact. The joys of being a self-righteous native are manifest and bounteous.

Casting a critical eye in the direction of others calls for some brief but thorough self-examination. There was a time when, as a lad, I engaged in some "angling" in the drainage that is not the sort of thing you'd read about in a book of Roderick Haig-Brown's. The day was August-perfect with the first hints of fall showing in the green aspen leaves now shading toward yellow. A couple of hours working a promising stretch of the creek went fishless, and frustration was building. Walking back to the truck, I noticed a spring creek pouring into the main stem and climbed over a fence to examine this water more closely. There were hundreds of pan-sized brook trout holding in the channels between the weed beds. The water was gin clear (I've always wanted to trot out this beat-up cliché) and not more than three feet deep. I knew I was on private property, but I believed that by crouching down I would be out of sight of anyone looking from the house a quarter of a mile upstream. Unlike its well-known cousins, Dupuy's and Armstrong, this little creek's fish were more than willing to pounce on my caddis. These guys were easy. After thirty minutes and thirty fish, or thereabouts, I crept farther upstream and discovered that the brookies had now been displaced by rainbows, some over a foot long. The fishing was a touch tougher with maybe a dozen in half an hour. Figuring I was tempting fate and maybe risking gunfire, I started off across the pasture toward the road and my truck.

Several rectangular ponds with raised banks confronted me. I thought they were for watering stock or storing water for the dry times of late summer, but when I kicked up a grasshopper that made the mistake of landing in one of these, the water boiled with hundreds of the blackest rainbow trout I'd ever seen. Dropping to my stomach along a bank, I plopped my fly in the pond and immediately countless trout attacked. This went on for some time. I could not help myself, and I must have caught (and released with great virtue) hundreds of pounds of rainbow. I was in a trance-like frenzy oblivious to my surroundings and would probably be buried there right now except for—

"Pretty durn easy to catch, ain't they?"

The shock of being discovered felt like an electric jolt in my guts. I slowly turned around to confront my fate, which I was sure would be defined by much ugliness and possibly violence.

"I've been watchin' your surreptitious antics for the past hour or so from down there." A nut-brown finger at the end of a very long arm indicated some irrigation pipe now shooting a silver-white spray over an emerald field a few hundred yards distant.

"Durn" and "surreptitious antics." I was in big trouble and all I could think of to say was "I'm sorry." I tried to leave.

"Where you goin'. You haven't kept any trout have you?" the deep voice queried. I was doomed. Jail, perhaps severe beatings. I'd just seen the artfully crafted film *Texas Chainsaw Massacre*, and my imagination was well into overdrive. "I've got ten bucks," I stammered, knowing this was no good.

"Keep your money," the voice boomed, and I saw death striding down from the dry hills to my right. "You ain't hurt nothin'. Go ahead and take a few of these, here. God-awful ugly fish, anyways."

Stunned, I did as I was ordered, watching from the nervous corners of my vision as the tall gentleman went back to his irrigating. I'd been saved—a reprieve granted from angling heaven. As crazy as the day was, I did actually keep a few of the trout and even took a photograph of one lying next to my bamboo rod on a gray log. That shot still hangs from my office wall as a reminder of the curious events and fortunes lying in wait out there for fly fishers.

Anyone familiar with Rock Creek will know where I am writing about, but I've already been far too specific and prefer to keep the incident's geographic details confined to a selective memory.

There are three general sections to the stream of about ten to fifteen miles each, and the different character and appearance of each is readily apparent. The first view of Rock Creek is from I-90 just before the Rock Creek exit, where the creek flows into the Clark Fork from the south, its banks lined with mature and quite large cottonwoods. This is beautiful water pouring over the coppery bed of rounded rocks, gravels, and down-sized boulders or sliding along undercut banks and weathered-gray tree trunks. The forested slopes of the Sapphire and Long John Mountains define the drainage winding into the distance as far as you can see. The scene looks like a hole on a very challenging golf course, but instead of lush green bent grass fairways you see cold pure water.

This is the beginning of the lower section, which is the most diverse of the trio with piles of logs, riffles, deep runs, pools, and the ever-popular undercut banks. Four-fifths of the trout population are browns, with the remainder predominantly rainbows of about one foot (and some measured in pounds holding down deep). There is also a smattering of cutts and bull trout. The browns are tough to catch (quite the revelation) and in some years make up less than half of the fish taken in this section. They will run in the fifteen- to eighteen-inch range, but as fall approaches substantially larger specimens move into Rock Creek from the Clark Fork as they begin their spawning runs. This is an opportunity to take trophy trout in a small-stream environment with the advantage of being able to determine where the prime holding areas are (unlike, say, portions of the Missouri where there is so much water that picking a location is mind boggling). The main problem lies in the fact that you are fishing in less water, which shrinks the area you have to play a hard-charging brown filled with procreational momentum. A five-pound fish can eat up a lot of space in seconds. Big nymphs, #2–4, and streamers fished down deep, often with a quick stripping retrieve, will entice the voracious attentions of these hefty guys. And there are times when small #14–18 patterns provide some entertainment. I've taken some healthy browns on Pheasant Tails and Partridge & Peacocks bounced along the bottom with sink-tip lines and often some weight, but the cost in tippet material and flies is awful, frightening beyond description.

This lower section has much private, posted land but is also accessible along the way from the oil-coated gravel road and from well-marked public access points. The valley is fairly wide and given over to some agrarian production such as hay fields, horse pastures, and well-manicured lawns replete with plastic pink flamingos (I'm serious). Rugged hills scarred by charcoal-gray scree slopes rise abruptly from the stream course. This is where you will find the majority of the anglers, including the bunch that likes to wade for bugs. Developed or not, though, this remains one beautiful trout stream.

The middle section tumbles through a narrow canyon and is about 60 percent rainbow, with lesser numbers of cutthroat and bull trout. The first two species are often taken in lengths of less than twelve inches, but because of the steep stream gradient and attendant fierce current, they are very feisty fish. The bull trout are a rarity averaging a couple of pounds but occasionally exceeding ten. This area is almost entirely fast-paced riffle, run, and swirling boulder water. Even with stream cleats and a wading staff, maneuvering without falling down is difficult. Adding to the sport are extremely clear water and trout with the best broken-water eyesight west of the Continental Divide. A crouching, cautious, measured approach is an absolute requirement and almost an impossibility in the slippery, convoluted, potentially ankle-fracturing bottom. I've gotten pretty wet here once or twice. Anything you catch in this water you've earned.

Elk Hair, Bucktail, and Goddard caddis; Goofus Bugs; Hare's Ear Nymphs; Zug Bugs; and the old Prince will take fish, as will stone fly nymphs and Sofa Pillows when the salmon flies are helicoptering through the air in late spring. I've also taken some nice trout dead-drifting a weighted Muddler Minnow in front of, past, and in back of midstream boulders all through the heat of day and particularly in the evening.

The upper section begins at the confluence of the East, West, and Ross's forks and is more meadow stream than anything else. Most of the best water snakes through posted private property with access occasionally granted (though on the decline) if you ask politely. The headwaters of Rock Creek pouring into this peaceful beginning are fed by snowmelt and springs tumbling down from rugged drainages in the Anaconda and Sapphire mountain ranges. I've never caught anything but pan-sized cutthroat and rainbows in this meandering, placid flow that you can almost jump over in spots, but there are always plenty of them that display a decided affinity for dry flies in the #14–18 range. Pattern selection is not a serious issue. This is typical open-meadow angling in a relatively high-altitude setting that is a delightful spot in which to spend an afternoon.

Something like 10,000 years ago when being a long-haired hipster was cool, my stepbrother and I did a lot of fishing at Rock Creek while supposedly pursuing an education at the University of Montana. This was back before the "blue-ribbon" frenzy hammered the trout, and we caught bunches of respectable fish. We used to tool up the interstate in a 1949 Ford Sportsman convertible—heavy wooden door panels, burgundy paint, leather interior, wide whitewalls, lots of chrome—a world-class fishing car in every sense of the concept. We did this almost every day around late afternoon and we always managed to pack a cooler with iced champagne—a gorgeous sight to behold—for the excursion. We were just a couple of irresponsible clowns with several years' worth of long hair hanging out beneath extremely wide-brimmed Stetsons. The good life.

We normally parked this spectacle alongside an excellent stretch of the water that was a few miles above Valley of the Moon, itself only minutes from I-90. There were (and still are) yards and yards of perfect riffles and glassy, deep runs only a few strides from the road, but they were completely isolated, out of sight of passing motorists. Foam-covered pools spun quietly in the shadows where dark-colored browns of size and distinction held sway. I've never come across better trout habitat anywhere. This was classic stuff that deserved the attention of bamboo rods, which we used with nothing but dries—not because we were purists. We simply did not know any other method of fly fishing. Nymphs and streamers were off in mysterious, uncharted, and unexplored country for us.

The pre-game ritual never varied. We'd rig up to the gentle sound of Papa John Creach's violin and the melodious machinations of the rest of Hot Tuna (a band of some renown in the early seventies) blasting from our dinosaur eight-track. After a glass or two of champagne, sipped stylishly, we calmly entered the water, my brother upstream to a favorite eddy and me directly across a gravel bank and over a miniature sand dune to some nice stuff sparkling beside a cut bank a few feet high.

There were always browns and rainbows over there eager to pounce on a Spruce Fly while there was still decent light and a White Miller as dusk drifted over the creek like velvet. Quartered upstream with a slight mend was all that was required in the way of a cast. The flies never covered more than a few yards of water before a fish was on. Three hundred feet of run along the bank at the most and never less than six or seven trout of fifteen inches and more. It was fabulous angling, available to the talents of anyone capable of throwing a line thirty feet.

After working this and maybe the pool leading to a logjam down below, I'd head back to the car, grab a fresh bottle of wine, and then walk quietly over to watch my brother, who by this time had taken some very nice browns out of "his" pool, usually back against a moss and grass overhang with a slight trickle of icy spring water seeping through. He'd finish and then we'd drain the bottle while drinking in Rock Creek at its finest, which back then (and maybe again some season soon) was all any fly fisher could ever want or imagine.

Clark Fork River (Upper Section)

*W*hat in the hell was that? It looked like a beaver—and then the dorsal fin and tail were visible and a head the size of a small dog's crashed through the water engulfing the Prince Nymph that up until then had been enjoying a relatively carefree float.

There was no need to set the hook. That was taken care of when the brown turned and swam straight across a serious current to its niche under some bushes beneath an undercut dirt bank. Yanking back on the light rod impressed the trout greatly, but, 2X tippet be damned, all the motion accomplished was the slightest twisting of its head and then, before the thing went even farther into the darkness, the snapping of the line on some submerged protrusion.

That was easily the biggest brown trout I'd ever hooked anywhere, much larger than the twenty-three-inch guy just released. Thirty inches sounds nice but is probably stretching the facts (though this has never been a concern of mine in the past, as several of my former daily newspaper editors will attest to), but twenty-seven inches or so is probably a slight underestimate.

I'd been casting away, jumping browns regularly, landing and releasing maybe half of them and missing the others on this stretch of the Clark Fork River well over an hour east of Missoula. I-90 was a few hundred yards in front of me, and catching good fish within sight and sound of that concrete madness was a pleasant juxtaposition of confused modern-day reality and unknown wonder. All of the browns were between seventeen and twenty-three inches. Really good fish. I'd measured each one just to be sure. But that last trout was huge, perhaps ten pounds, and when it first turned for the fly I thought the large splash was just a variance in the current as the river rushed over a mossy rock. Then I thought I'd spooked a beaver or muskrat until I saw otherwise.

The connection was brief yet long enough to render my hands shakingly useless, so I staggered back to shore to settle down. The upper Clark Fork has always been good brown trout water despite pollution problems from past mining operations that have rendered fish flesh toxic and hence of no value to meat fishermen. The other trout were slightly larger than I normally took along here but not really anomalies. That last brown was stunning, something I never expected to come across in this stretch of the river. Even if a six- or seven-weight rod was involved instead of a four-weight the outcome would have been the same. That was just too much fish in too little water. The whole run could be waded in hippers with room to spare.

The Clark Fork flows for almost 300 miles before leaving the state west of Heron and heading into Idaho. For the sake of arbitrariness, the upper half begins at Turah, a few minutes east of Missoula and above where the Blackfoot River enters. This stretch runs almost to Anaconda and is well over 125 miles long. The river more or less has its headwaters at Warm Springs Creek within sight of "the world's largest stack," which on a daily basis used to discharge into the air tons of pollutants resulting from copper smelting from its sixty-foot-wide mouth almost 600 feet above ground. The structure, an impressive, malevolent reminder of the state's past, has been inactive for years. Where Silver Bow Creek joins forces with Warm Springs, and then for nearly twenty miles downstream, healthy numbers of browns can be picked up in mostly shallow water that is twenty feet wide. You'll catch fish, but the area is a dumping ground for mine tailings whose history dates back to the days before the turn of the century, when copper really drove the state's fortunes.

The upper Clark Fork suffers from the dumping of mining wastes for its entire length, along with discharges of private and municipal sewage. While many of the problems have been lessened or eliminated altogether, much of the river is barren or holds few fish. Adding to an angler's difficulties is the fact that each year's runoff flushes away some of the toxic crud and revives the streambed in a given area. Aquatic insects begin to come back, along with the browns. The nature and health of the river is in a constant state of flux, and knowing where to fish is a year-to-year problem. One good bit of advice is to work below the mouths of any creeks or streams that enter the river. These waters provide a constant cleansing of the river, and trout normally are found in this type of wholesome situation.

To add to this delightful picture, the sewage feeds the algae (moss) that creates oxygen to saturation levels during the day. The oxygen usually dissipates at night and then builds up again the next day. These up-and-down variations do a number on the trout. Water temperatures in some areas reach eighty degrees during the heat of summer, which also has deleterious effects. Stream channelization that took place when the interstate highway was constructed has laid waste to long pieces of formerly fine fishing water. Along the upper Clark Fork, you have to pick your spots, and this is now often a hit-or-miss proposition.

A typical and all-too-common situation occurred in the summer of 1989. Montana's extractive mining past caught up with the river, as it has so many times in recent years. Heavy thunderstorms on Wednesday, July 12, dumped over an inch of rain on the Deer Lodge Valley in a few hours (a not uncommon occurrence in western Montana) during the afternoon and evening, leading to the poisonous deluge of discarded mining tailings in an area that is part of the site of the nation's largest Superfund cleanup. Thousands of trout, including many of the huge browns, were destroyed by the torrential runoff filled with deadly amounts of toxic heavy metals accumulated from previous

Fishing the upper Clark Fork River.

mining operations in the Butte area. The fish population (browns, rainbows, cutthroat, whitefish, and forage fish) still has not recovered and may not for years.

A survey following the kill revealed that a total of 5,290 fish died, including 2,270 brown trout that averaged eleven inches and three-quarters of a pound. The largest brown was two feet long. Almost 700 whitefish were also killed. Recent Montana Department of Fish, Wildlife and Parks (MDFWP) data indicate that portions of this seventeen-mile stretch of water had held between 1,500 and 2,000 catchable brown trout per mile.

The tailings area is a result of extensive mining operations begun in the 1860s at "the richest hill on earth" at Butte. The hill, now called the Berkeley Pit, is a mile wide and averages 1,000 feet deep. An estimated 185 million cubic yards of contaminated earth taken from that hole now rests as tailings in an area that stretches from Butte to Anaconda twenty miles to the west. Anyone traveling along I-90 as the highway passes through Butte only has to look to the north to see the extent of this excavation.

In 1954 the Anaconda Company began steps to limit downstream discharges, which included construction of the Warm Springs pond. Anaconda Company ceased all operations in Montana in the mid-1970s, leaving the deadly tailings behind when it pulled up stakes. Superfund legislation in 1986 was designed to prevent the river from "running red" with toxic waste in the future.

Dry weather after spring runoff causes copper and zinc compounds from mine tailings to leach to the surface of stream banks, where they appear as a greenish-blue precipitate. A moderate amount of rain soaks toxins back into the soil where they will not harm trout populations, but this storm's output was not completely absorbed by the soil, and the poisons entered the river and clogged the gills of the fish, leading to a gruesome death by asphyxiation. Following the latest kill, fish littered the stream course, white belly up, for miles.

"We have fish dying from Warm Springs all the way to the Deer

Lodge area," said Glenn Phillips, pollution-control biologist with the MDFWP, immediately after the kill.

The toxic tailings have washed down Silver Bow Creek and accumulated in the affected area. Phillips attributes the fish kill to a combination of the previous summer's drought, 1989's late spring, and the intensity of the storm.

"We've been looking at ways to manage the whole system for a couple of years," Phillips said. "From my perspective there will have to be some sort of removal and stabilization of the tailings to prevent this from happening again." He added that he anticipates some type of solution will be hammered out with state officials in the future, but an even bigger problem may be finding a site for the tailings when they are removed from the Clark Fork drainage.

"What you're talking about here is an acute situation," said MDFWP information officer Bill Thomas. "We're attempting to document what happened. Depending upon the extent of the damage, it will be at least several years before the brown trout population returns to its former level.

"The stream had really come back well and if you could look past some of the aesthetics [resulting from past mining activities], this was probably one of the best stretches of brown trout water in the state." These "aesthetics" include the visual blight of the tailings and an acrid smell that is especially noticeable on warm, humid (by Montana standards) days.

Region 1 fisheries manager Jim Vashro said that as of the first of August 1989, some brown trout had been reported in the affected section of the river. Vashro believes these fish were survivors of the kill and fish that moved up from downstream into holding areas.

I realize that reading about this is not as entertaining as tales of catching leviathan browns, but what happened here is an all-too-common scenario throughout the West. To date, little has changed concerning this situation on the upper Clark Fork. The piles of toxic metals still lie baking in the sun waiting for the next downpour. You'll notice mile upon mile of them as you drive by on the interstate. The only hope for the river's fishery and the river itself, in the long run, is to completely remove the mine tailings.

A number of ghost towns hiding out in the hills around the upper section of the Clark Fork are spectral reminders of this harsh past and often destructive present. Garnet, Coloma, Bearmouth, and Beartown are all part of the Bear Gulch drainage, and each has its own wild and usually bizarre tales to tell.

The following episode took place in Beartown and is pretty much representative of the behavior exhibited by the local inhabitants a hundred years or so ago. The incident, described by Muriel Sibell Wolle in *The Bonanza Trail,* concerned a Dr. Armistead "Mit" Mitchell of nearby Deer Lodge, who traveled to Beartown on occasion for a drink and some medical practice. Drunk or sober, the guy apparently could do his job.

One morning he arrived at Abascal's store to perform an operation on Shorty, who had the misfortune, while dead drunk, to stumble into his own fireplace and lie down with his arm in the embers all night until it was burned to a crisp. As soon as "Mit" had sawed off the arm and bound up the stump in a soiled rag, Shorty, still fortified against pain by whiskey, ran to the door and called in his friends for a round of drinks. While the boys crowded around the patient, "Mit" collected the scraps of flesh and bone and put them in a gunny sack to take home, with some fuzzy idea of using them in an experiment he was conducting. The board and two whiskey barrels that had served as the operating table were put away, and Shorty, the doctor, and two or three cronies sat down to an all day game of poker. That evening a dance was held at Pelletier's [saloon] and everyone went. It was daylight when it broke up, and the doctor lurched to his horse, carrying the sack of charred bones. Somewhere along the trail he lost the arm.

Despite this sordid history of craziness, destruction, and neglect, what is truly amazing (Warning! Trout-fishing hyperbole ahead!) is the brown trout fishing that still exists in this beleaguered water.

A couple of months after the latest heavy-metal-inspired dieoff I drove down to this section of poorly treated water to see for myself if any trout were still around or had moved back into the water, as Vashro mentioned. The guy knows his water or has very good sources of information or both, because the browns were here.

They averaged about a foot and looked healthy: firm, full-bodied, and colorful. Tempted by an Elk Hair Caddis and a Goddard Caddis (this one exclusively in fast water), over a dozen fish leaped up from their holding areas against the willow-covered banks, from behind rocks, and in the riffles to snap at the high-floating imitations. To take this many fish in water that had been devastated earlier that summer was amazing and a testament (I truly do believe) to the incredible ability the Clark Fork has to bounce back from continual mistreatment. I can only imagine what the fishing would be like if the water ever had twenty or thirty years to heal itself. Browns to ten pounds everywhere.

If you can ignore a smell that is reminiscent of a raunchy version of the vapors venting out of the earth at Yellowstone National Park, everything along this poisoned stretch of the river seems normal. The heaps of discarded tailings are for the most part invisible, lurking behind thick, brushy growth along the banks. The Flint Creek Range, now showing off a mantle of fresh snow, sparkles on the western horizon. Tan-, brown- and gray-colored hills roll off toward Butte in the east. The water is clear and sparkling in the sunlight and looks pure and drinkable as it tumbles over the bright browns, yellows, and oranges of the streambed. Appearances are deceiving, however. This looks like a charming, productive little trout stream, which in many respects it still is, despite the toxic nature of its water. If you drank a quart of the liquid, you would have another, sickly impression. The water would not kill you and probably would cause only a small but noticeable pain in your gut, but its burden of heavy metals would be forever stored in your body's tissues. Accumulate too much and you die. I think of the browns living here and hope that perhaps someday the river will be clean and pure again.

Most of the times when success has been an angling companion here, large patterns have been a part of the equation: Prince Nymphs, Buggers, Montana Stones, Spruce Flies, Bitch Creeks, Girdle Bugs, Yuk Bugs, and sculpin patterns. Large hoppers have produced in July and August. In the evenings of summer and early autumn, caddis imitations and similar patterns will often take plenty of trout, but the big stuff is more consistent.

Fishing the river below the Superfund site near Warm Springs can be excellent when the prolific caddis hatches come off. Emergers and then dries can take a number of fat browns that rise in abundance along the brushy, tree-lined streamcourse. The fishing can be difficult, and the right pattern and a delicate, accurate presentation is everything. When I first began hanging around the Clark Fork I used to cast small dries up and across the water with much back-and-forth waving of the rod. The fly always looked very nice bouncing along on top of the river, but I never caught anything. And then one day a game warden checking licenses on the river told me that "the fish here don't go for that little shit. . . . They pretty much stick to the big stuff and you should, too, if you want to do any more than practice your casting."

Learning how to work large patterns down deep took years and is an ongoing process that yields some new piece of information, if only on a subconscious level, every time out. The more I learn, the more I realize how little I understand about the process.

The most curious fishing for a single trout in a specific location dealing with precisely defined feeding habits concerns a guy who sold me my first bamboo rod years ago in Missoula. This individual was locally known as an excellent fly caster and taker of big trout. One day when I entered his shop along the Clark Fork in the center of town I observed that he was tying a white butterfly pattern. Since there was also a bottle of Jack Daniels on the bench, I figured this behavior was of the flight-of-fancy variety, but he assured me that there was a large brown feeding along a bank above Clinton that was taking the butterflies whenever they fluttered too close to the water. Back in those days of crazed-hipster behavior I had weird concepts of my own that needed supervision, so I purchased some flies and headed back to the hills. I didn't need to start chasing trout with butterflies.

Some weeks later I returned to the shop and asked for an update on the situation. I was shown the large white-winged pattern, now totally worked over and looking like it had been in a bar fight.

"Fly like this is only good for one cast and it had to be perfect," my friend said. "It was and that brown came out from under the bank and took the sucker right off. Ran downstream like crazy, but I finally got him to me."

That was all he ever told me about the experience, but I did hear from a mutual acquaintance, long since gone from the planet, that the brown was thirty inches, minimum, hefty, and way over ten pounds.

Next year I'll give the concept a try some hot July afternoon. The whole idea sounds pretty good while sitting here watching the rain come down.

Butterflies on the Clark Fork. . . . Why not? Everything else has happened on this river.

Big Hole River

*T*he Big Hole River. The mere mention of this famous southwestern Montana water conjures febrile images of browns and rainbows staggering in their numbers and heroic in size. Tales of the fishing on this stream run off in unchecked, hyperbolic overdrive, careening around sedate, steeply banked curves of angling reality before roaring wildly out of control down starkly lonesome straightaways of truth and believable information. Exhaust from this madness lingers beneath a white-hot August sky.

Oh yes, there are trophy trout swimming in deep pools and holding hard in dark, protected water beneath downed cottonwoods. Cannibalistic fervor sends imperceptible flickers of excitement shivering down their muscular flanks. The truly huge fish of the river live only to eat, to devour the smaller of their species and sculpins, too.

The eager stories of fly fishers tell how these trout are caught so frequently that one wonders what need exists for skills associated with the chase. These reports swirl around the state with hypnotic rhythms like a riverine eddy spinning thick foam galaxies. There are so many fish here, the voices say, that everyone will catch the five-pounder of haunted dreams. And if the trout fail to cooperate with size, the recalcitrance will be corrected with frenzied abundance. Dozens of trout in smaller dimensions will strike on every cast. By evening, questions of why fish the Big Hole more than once will be asked. This is so easy and so pure an angling epiphany that it needs to be experienced only once and then carefully filed away in memory for comparison with the lesser waters of the world. Why bother to come back?

Why bother? I'll tell you why, damn it!

We've been floating on this water for hours under a mean sun, flies buzzing around our heads and eating chunks of our flesh. The beer in the cooler passed lukewarm two bends in the river ago and has a bitter taste. All we've caught are three anemic rainbows of maybe eight inches each—real big fish. One streamer is dragging half in and half out of the water, and the leader makes fantastic silhouetted shapes against the horizon while hanging languidly from a rod tip, twisted and knotted beyond salvation. The other rig is already broken down (as we all are in the raft) and tucked away in a metal tube. Our guide finally gave up being optimistic a few minutes back and is guzzling beer. Amber liquid and white suds run down his chin and stain his brightly colored shirt. The scarred, wooden oars drag lazily in the current. We are going nowhere and have accepted our deserved situation. Landing at the takeout, removing our waders, and heading into town for a sizzling, thick, very rare steak and an icy beverage are dreams of choice and possible realization. Drifting beneath towering formations of rock, we see goats maneuvering among vertiginous outcroppings far above, almost invisible, kicking loose rivulets of stones that bounce and clatter down to the water: sedimentary music for the piscatorially damned. In this heat, the moist, fertile essence of the river is pervasive, maddening. There is no wind. Not a puff to clear the air. This is the oblivion express, salmonid style.

"Where are the damned trout, John?" my stepfather wonders.

"Don't ask him. He hasn't moved a fish all day," the guide offers between gulps of beer.

"All you touched were some whitefish. People must pile in from all over the world for that privilege," I add, and we float on, now speechless, stunned, staring at the country through bloodshot eyes, wondering where the fish are.

They are here, but the big ones are down in number and still dropping. Dry years, heavy irrigation demands, and tens of thousands of anglers working the river have seen to that. The browns are faring somewhat better than the rainbows, but both species experience a lot of attention from us during the salmon fly hatch in June, which is also a time of high water from snowmelt in the surrounding Beaverhead, Pioneer, and Anaconda Mountains. Most people concentrate their efforts on the thirty-mile stretch between Wise River and Glen. Even at times of heavy runoff the Big Hole does not muddy up like other rivers in the state. Sofa Pillows bounced along the surface or a Montana Stone Nymph 2X or 4X dredged across the bottom take trout with frequency. It is best to be a little ahead of the hatch, which wanders upstream several miles each day. Wherever you are on the water, expect dozens of boats, crowds on the shore, and general mayhem. After a few days of this silliness, the trout are wary and not so willing to chase a fly. Look at things this way: If every time you stepped out the front door, someone winged a baseball at you, how long would it take before you realized that lounging in the recliner watching reruns of "The Brady Bunch" was much the safer (and intellectually superior) life?

After about mid-July the water level stabilizes and a good portion of the crowd has turned its frantic attentions to other western rivers. There are still plenty of anglers working the river, but you have opportunities to pick and choose places that offer solitude and, as in our case described earlier, disillusionment.

The Big Hole's reputation as world-class trout water is deserved, but for some reason on some days the river shuts down and no one can take decent fish with any consistency. Return a few days later and the surface will be alive with feeding trout of all sizes. A few more days down the calendar, the trout will seem to have vanished from the face of the earth. Perhaps the irrigation demands of ranchers upstream trigger some sort of subtle chemical change in the river, whose normally high pH level contributes greatly to abundant moss and algae growth. This growth makes nymphing and wading difficult, but the greenery also creates an excellent habitat for aquatic life forms like caddis, stone flies, and sculpins.

Pattern selection is not as critical as it is on, say, Nelson's Spring Creek over by Yellowstone. An assortment of Royal Wulffs, Humpies, hoppers, Adams, Goofus Bugs, Henryvilles, and Elk Hair Caddis will cover most of the dry-fly action. Bitch Creeks, Girdle Bugs, Woolly Buggers, Marabou Muddlers, and sculpins can handle the big stuff down deep. For nymphs, the Prince, Hare's Ear, and Zug Bugs have their moments. Some rivers, like the Beaverhead and the North Fork of the Flathead, have specific techniques that out-fish all others combined when you are seeking trophies, but a variety of methods works on the Big Hole. In one stretch you can use dries, drag nymphs along the bottom, and then hammer the water with streamers, and there is a good chance of taking fish each way within an hour.

From Glen down to Twin Bridges the river runs deeper and slower and browns predominate, feeding on sculpins, whitefish, and smaller rainbows. When streamflow has not been disrupted by excessive irrigation, the fishing can be very good. Unfortunately, by August the river is down and warming daily. The big boys have gone off in search of out-of-the-way springs and some cool shade. The Big Hole really is a great river, even with its off days, but gluttonous water usage is seriously damaging the stream for much of its more than 100 miles of length. Some ranchers in the valley believe that because they were granted water rights decades ago before the value of the trout resource was recognized, they have the inalienable right to use every drop entitled to them, regardless of need. This greedy, shortsighted behavior needs to be legislated back to the dark ages where it originated.

Forget this area until autumn. Then work it hard with the likes of Matuka Sculpins and Woolly Buggers. Fishing the Bugger is not glamorous but probably accounts for more big fish than any other pattern in Montana. Worked diligently, with extremely fast strips and bank-tight, the response this thing provokes in big browns is insane. Whip the pattern right off the bank and start stripping as fast as you can while the Bugger is still coming down. Big browns will race out from the bank in mad rushes. You'll miss more than you connect with, but the action is invigorating. Given the limitations of using just one pattern for the rest of my life, the selection would be the Woolly Bugger. Five years ago the picks were an Adams or Muddler or maybe a Hare's Ear.

All of the water described so far is worthy of anyone's attention, but the upper basin way on past Wisdom near Jackson is my favorite part of the river. Mountain men of times past referred to this type of deep valley as a "hole," which indirectly led to the naming of the river. Lewis and Clark were probably the first white guys to see this part of the country. Wandering through lush green hay fields, you'll see dozens of bizarre contrivances that look like very weird looms. They are called beaverslides and are used to put up this wealth of hay. Small willows protect the banks. The Big Hole is an unspoiled little beauty.

The Big Hole—really just a brook in the basin with mountains and dark pine forest looking down from all directions—is prime holding water for the last significant stream-dwelling population of arctic grayling in the lower forty-eight states. Proposed logging in the drainage threatens to eliminate even these few wild fish. They used to be common in the Missouri River and its tributaries above Great Falls (in 1805, the Lewis and Clark expedition referred to them as a "new kind of white or silvery trout"), but logging and development eliminated that population (radical Trout Polemics are vibrating close by in the hills).

Chasing grayling has been an avocation of mine for years, ever since I saw people fishing for them in Alaska in old black-and-white home movies taken in the late thirties. Their signature feature is a large sail-like dorsal fin with irregular yet distinct rows of turquoise spots. The other fins usually show a yellowish cast, and the pelvic fins often have lengthwise stripes of black and pink. When you catch one, its colors intensify and seem to trip into fluorescence like a freshwater marlin.

Fishing the Big Hole River.

They are scaly, silver-bodied fish shading to purple with trout-like heads tapering to small mouths. In some ways they resemble mountain whitefish. They do not grow large; a grayling of just under six pounds taken in the Northwest Territories sets the standard. Two pounds is a trophy in Montana, but larger ones are taken occasionally.

The Latin name *Thymallus arcticus* comes from the species' supposed thymelike smell, which I've never been able to detect, though a number of my friends mistakenly believe that you must sniff a grayling before you release it. The few I've kept for the table have proven excellent fare when poached in a little butter and white wine. The excellent quality of the flesh was one of the major reasons for the extinction of grayling in Michigan by the 1940s. The poor things were hauled from the water in massive numbers to be shipped to gourmet establishments back East. Many of them wound up rotting in the sun beside the railroad tracks when trains failed to arrive on schedule.

The last ice age in North America wiped out many species when the huge glaciers ground their way south. As the climate began to heat up again, warmwater species returned, but the grayling were here all along, swimming in the open rivers and lakes right up to the edge of the towering fields of ice. Over the millennia they evolved into an elongated, muscular shape perfect for fast current. The large, sweeping dorsal fin provides the stability needed to forage in this fast-paced environment.

The last time I chased these fish unfortunately can be measured in years and not in weeks. As usual, a late start was the order of the day, and it was well past noon when I began casting a small Adams through fast-paced runs that held feeding grayling. The fish were easy to catch and zipped back and forth in the current when hooked. A two-weight rod was ideal for this fishing, and a foot-long grayling was good sport.

Even in moving water they will hold near the bottom and then rocket almost straight up to the surface to take a fly. In lakes where they have been stocked you can see them coming from a long way down, silver missiles blasting up through their heavy, emerald atmosphere, slamming your dry, and then screaming back down to cover. The displeasure they display when hooked—head shakings and angry little runs—is so obvious that you soon begin to feel quite guilty about the situation, which adds another layer of experience to your sport.

Several people have told me of separate incidents in which grayling have leaped out of the water trying to take flies dangling from the tips of rods put aside near a stream. All of these incidents occurred in Alaska, and I have never observed these antics in Montana, but I have spent a few moments trying to duplicate the results on this stretch of the Big Hole—with no luck.

As I mentioned earlier, the river can be fabulous fishing, and this knowledge keeps me coming back despite several outings of indifference and few fish. Perhaps working the water from shore will change things, I think. Careful stalking approaches, and delicate but swift and accurate casts that drop small dries above feeding trout surely must generate results. Walking well away from the bank, I spot a pod of browns working quietly in some slack, tea-colored water along the shore. The only indication of current is the slight ripples behind rocks blocking the flow. The fish shift from side to side with easy swingings of their tails. Sipping diminutive caddis looks effortless for the big browns. A dozen or more of them are spread out through the run. Every fish is hefty, wide near the head.

Crouching down, I work to within twenty feet of the water and reach casting position behind a medium-sized boulder that is covered with the exo-skeletons of salmon flies from earlier this season. False-casting until I have the water covered for the first trout, I artfully let fly with an effort that settles on the water with a certain degree of finesse, I think, but I am proved wrong as the first three browns stop feeding. I sadly watch the V-shape of their wakes pointing to deeper water. The next cast produces similar results, and within a half-dozen drifts, all of the browns are safely resting out of sight in the middle of the river. This is perhaps one of the most devastating angling experiences imaginable.

There are times when I think I really know how to catch trout with a fly. Times when everything seems to click, when all the nuance, subtlety, and artifice seem to function as one concept—a single, smooth-flowing series of actions. Times when taking large fish is easy and joyous.

Then there are my experiences on the lower Big Hole, a river where I cannot seem to do anything right. This is a frustrating and often depressing place for me. Why are the river's fish so difficult to take? What am I doing wrong? Perhaps my timing is off, or the moon is in a weird phase, or I should be eating more tofu instead of red meat. I just do not know what's going on where the Big Hole is concerned.

I'm lost, but I will always find my way back to this river . . . .

Beaverhead River

*W*hen my thoughts turn toward fast-paced, difficult, and challenging fishing in Montana, images of the willow-choked banks and cruising runs of the Beaverhead flash through my mind like a crazy, slightly out-of-focus, somewhat pleasurable nightmare. My experiences on this intriguing river are humbling, educational, occasionally productive, and always rewarding.

This is not the kind of angling so often associated with Montana mountain streams. This is trout hardball in big-league fashion. Factor into this equation the increasingly common hardships caused by a lack of adequate moisture in the region, resulting in very low stream flows, and you have the scenario for tough, frustrating angling.

Few will argue that getting a hit off Nolan Ryan during the peak of the game is a bit difficult for the gifted professional ballplayer. But let's say the diamond powers-that-be all of a sudden add fifteen miles per hour to his fastball and an even more wicked break to his slider. Now you are talking serious business. Full-time concentration is required.

Well, that's the Beaverhead. What was once tough fishing is now even more difficult. Some very good fly fishers have spent some very long, unproductive days on this water in the past few years.

Tuck casts, mending the line in the air with a pair of weighted nymphs homing on the back of a balding head, pinpoint casts to minuscule pockets that rush past in an instant, maintaining constant contact with a couple of down-deep flies that seem to have their own ideas on what constitutes a proper drift, and trout that display an epicurean discrimination are all part of the course. Fishing and catching trout on the Beaverhead is not for everyone. It requires specific skills—which any fly fisher can master over a period of time with dedicated practice.

The Beaverhead demands the best from an individual, and even that is frequently insufficient. Yet if I were limited to one water for the rest of my life it would be this crafty amalgamation of undercut banks, runs, riffles, and pools. As a friend of mine said recently, "If you can catch fish on the Beaverhead, you can catch them anywhere."

His statement proved true on a recent trip of mine to a difficult-to-fish stream in central Montana. Using techniques I learned on the wicked, wicked Beaverhead, I produced trout while others went fishless using different methods.

The Beaverhead is famous for very big trout that are often taken with the old "chuck-and-duck" method of hammering large, weighted streamers tight to the bank and then rapidly stripping them back to you. And of course there are the prolific hatches of caddis, pale morning duns, little yellow stones, and those monstrous parodies of mosquitoes, crane flies, that provide quality action on dries. All of this, wrapped in proud and frequently unproductive tradition, still has a vital role in the angling rhythms of this elaborate river. Patterns imitating these creatures take many large fish every season.

The Beaverhead is undergoing a surprisingly swift change, however. And those of us who fail to pick up on this subtle shift, or are too damn set in our ways to adapt, might as well turn our angling attentions elsewhere, especially when the current problems are also factored in. Guides, fisheries biologists, and even slightly myopic writers have noticed the change, and the consensus is that to consistently take large trout on the river you must use nymphs, down deep.

"It's not really a Woolly Bugger river anymore," said Tim Tollett of

Frontier Anglers in Dillon. "You can still catch big fish that way, but they see so many buggers and dry flies that they have become extremely selective. Even when somebody's home in a good hole and you make a perfect cast and retrieve, the trout will not always take. A good drift with a couple of nymphs will outfish any other method, by far. Using a Partridge & Peacock on the point and an Antron as a dropper is one of the best combinations I've found."

This observation was backed up by state fisheries biologist Dick Oswald, who said, "The overall trend in the last nine years has been away from 'crude' fishing with Girdle Bugs and 15–20-pound tippets whacked to the bank. The big and ugly stuff used to hold sway, but it is not very often that you do well with that now."

According to Oswald, pattern selection has become more varied, and the size has gone way down in part because the fish are seeing an increase in pressure from anglers.

"I know a lot of guys who were very good at taking big fish on the big stuff, but they've gone through troubled times, and some still haven't adapted," Oswald added. "There's no question that some people have tailored their methods [to the changing conditions] and are very successful."

The Beaverhead flows north through irrigated pastureland in southwestern Montana. Rolling hills staggered with rugged rock formations flank the river. As the light changes throughout the day you will see a multitude of colors and their shadings kaleidoscoping around you. The Pioneer Range to the west and the Ruby Range to the east are not visible when floating the upper stretch, which contains the best trophy trout water.

Lewis and Clark once thought that this headwater of the Missouri might be a convenient passage to the promised land along the Pacific Coast. Further examination proved otherwise. (For some reason you just cannot float a raft over the crest of the Northern Rockies.)

The tailrace of the Clark Canyon Dam, completed in 1964, now forms the beginning of the Beaverhead. The river is dependent on

Nymphing the Beaverhead in August.

water releases from the dam to maintain an adequate flow and temperature for big fish. Releases, though fluctuating in nature, ensure sufficient flows of cold water, habitat for the fecund trout population. The immediate effects of runoff and summer snowmelt are not as dramatic here as in other rivers of the Rocky Mountain West.

Under so-called ideal conditions, starting in May the rate of flow rises to around 500–700 cfs, compared to winter rates in the 200–250 range (flows have dropped into the 35–50 cfs range over the last few winters). During the height of the irrigation season in June and July the flow rises to 900–1,100 and then drops back down to 600–700 in August.

When I mentioned to Oswald that I had experienced a tough time fishing on my last visit to the river, the biologist said, "Don't feel like the Lone Ranger. In that upper section [from the tailrace to Barrett's Diversion], six to eight fish is a good day for me."

What makes this tough to take is the knowledge that literally tons of trout are present in periods of adequate water flow in every mile of water. A ballpark figure would be 2,500 pounds of browns and 1,500 pounds of rainbows per mile. Two tons of trout waiting to be caught!

Oswald, not completely comfortable with this figure, prefers to cite 550 trout of eighteen inches and up per mile. He described a classic example of the frustrating nature of the Beaverhead.

"There's one stretch of bank covered in willows that, for the angler, is essentially dead," he said. "I asked one biologist if he'd ever caught a fish there and he said, 'No.' But when we have to shock [survey] this stretch no one wants to handle the net. It's not possible to bring to net all of the fish. Your arms will give out before you can haul in all of those trout."

Many serious fly fishers consider the Beaverhead to be one of the top trophy trout waters in the world, but for the river to maintain this status some serious flow problems need to be addressed. Extremely low water flows are hammering the populations of big browns and rainbows. Special regulations are now in effect because of the sharp drop in trout numbers caused by the low water levels, particularly those of the 1988–1989 winter. The drought has eased its deadly grip on many waters of the West recently, but severe low-moisture conditions have plagued the Beaverhead on a regular basis since the 1987 season.

The Bureau of Reclamation, which controls the Clark Canyon Dam, which in turn controls the amount of water released from Clark Canyon Reservoir into the Beaverhead, has guaranteed a minimum flow of between 35 and 50 cubic feet per second. Even with this "generous" flow, the river still lost over half of its twenty-inch or larger browns and a similar number of rainbows.

Oswald says that at least 140 cfs is needed to maintain winter populations. Clark Canyon storage has been down more often than not when cold weather arrives, and the heavy snows needed to recharge the moisture system have not been forthcoming. At least three years of average to above-average precipitation is needed to start the recovery process, and even more time is needed to reestablish good numbers of healthy fish.

For those of us who put a river and a trout's well-being ahead of our sport, a 1989 survey by the Montana Department of Fish, Wildlife and Parks (MDFWP) is alarming. Densities of over-twenty-inch browns were down to 150 per mile, over-eighteen-inch browns experienced a 38 percent decline, over-twenty-inch fish were down 58 percent, and the condition of the remaining big trout showed a 16 percent drop in body weight. More water more consistently released is badly needed. Water is the blood of a river. Without it, the river dies.

Recent regulations that are designed to mitigate the problem include the imposition of a three-fish limit from the dam down to Dillon, and only one fish over eighteen inches may be kept. Previously, there had been a five-fish limit with one over eighteen inches in possession, and the sight of bait fishermen hauling away trophy browns on stringers was not uncommon.

"While this is cause for concern, the river has an incredible capacity to bounce back," said Oswald. "During shocking [surveys in past years of abundance] in the spring and fall I handle a hell of a lot of fish between five and ten pounds and a few of the bizarre monsters up to fifteen pounds."

Browns make up about 70 percent and rainbows around 30 percent of the numbers of catchable trout. The size of the fish shows a gradual decline as you move downriver toward Dillon to the north, and the number of rainbows falls off to just 5 percent near town.

With a river current sometimes greater than five miles per hour and deep, swirling holes exceeding ten feet, you don't have much time to plan your cast and drift. A quick glance ahead to ascertain the next pocket and then an almost instinctive cast dead tight to the bank is required.

On one float I cast a Partridge & Peacock point fly and an Antron dropper (an emerger imitation) next to the willows as we flew over a rocky shelf just above a good hole. A trout solidly took, and before I had a chance to react (time has slowed my near-legendary reflexes), the fish was forty feet upstream near the bank, broken off—angling history.

The bite of the hook had caused him to leap twice heading upstream. This was a big fish, a brown well over twenty-four inches and very thick. Tollett commented throughout the rest of the day that the fish "was easily over seven pounds. Too bad you lost him." A pair of sandhill cranes clacked away in derision from a nearby gravel bar. Nice guy, that Tollett, but he was right. It was a good fish even though our connection was somewhat brief in nature. (It has been a couple of years since that incident and I still hear from this compassionate man that "I caught a damn nice brown the other day, but nowhere near as big as that hog you lost.")

That's another difficulty with fishing here. When you do tie into a nice fish, you are usually heading fast, fast, fast downriver while the trout is doing the same routine in the opposite direction. Getting the raft beached quickly and jumping out in hot pursuit is often as much a matter of luck and good timing as skill. Because you're rolling down the river at such a rapid clip, casts must angle downstream, made with a quick, mid-air upstream mend. And they must be tight to the bank so that when they sink they have not pulled back in too close to the raft and away from the holding areas.

Weight, often two or more twist-ons, is needed to get the nymphs down quickly. This requirement adds to the casting excitement for angler and guide alike. Tollett has this technique down to an art. I don't, but by the end of the first day I was making a few well-executed casts out of what seemed like thousands. Rotator-cuff surgery was lurking at every bend in the river.

With the combined weight of the flies and lead, picking the line smartly off the water and back high above you is necessary. Tucking the line back down accurately and almost completely extended takes a little practice. Tollett suggested that when I feel the weight of the line begin to load the rod I imagine casting a lure on an ultralight spinning rod and the action needed to propel the lure to the intended spot. This quick, forceful, and abrupt downward motion, when executed properly, has the same feel as pulling down on a small, pliant tree limb. You'll know when you're doing this properly because the cast will lay out across the water's surface like a frozen rope and your flies will hit with audible and visible plops.

This method is far from delicate or graceful, and it may border on heretical to fly fishing purists, but it is extremely effective for making fish-producing presentations on the Beaverhead. Catching trout in these circumstances is, to some degree, work, and it demands aggressive techniques.

First observations of someone experienced in this type of angling create the false impression that little skill or finesse is involved. Nothing could be farther from the true reality of the situation. Learning to read the water at a glance and programming the mind and muscles to react instantly, and then actually slamming the cast within an inch of the bank, often with a sidearm motion to slip under overhanging willow branches, is an art. Reflexes and concentration are everything. Hitting Nolan Ryan's sharp-breaking slider is no more difficult.

Even after a perfect cast is made, maintaining full contact with your leader is a constant process. Look away or drift off mentally for just a fraction of a second, and the presentation reveals its artificial nature to the trout. The drift is wasted.

If you cast right-handed, gaining control of the line under that hand's index finger means quickly moving the line with the left hand. If this quick shift is not done, control is diminished and the productivity of the cast is greatly reduced.

Leaning over the raft, extending your arm straight out, raising and lowering the rod as depth varies, and mending line all come into play on almost every cast. The weight must bounce along the bottom, but sufficient tension is needed to detect strikes and to drift the nymphs through a run in a free, natural way. A correct drift will transmit the slightest amount of heft and resistance back up through the line and to your hand.

"Once you get the hang of this, and you will in time," added Tollett as he made a nice cast with my rod, "you can add one more dimension to the cast. While the line is suspended in the air for that brief moment, throw a quick little upstream mend in it. This can make all the difference between catching and not catching fish. Those added inches of drift the mend gives you are crucial."

This mend is accomplished with a quick flick of the rod upstream and an almost simultaneous dropping of your elbow and then rod tip. The movement is only a matter of inches, but the results can be dramatic. I'll be the first to admit that this technique approaches exertion on both the physical and mental planes, which was not part of the original angling plan many years ago, but the results justify the effort. Futile flinging of flylines and flies hour after hour on the water is not my idea of big-time fun.

Tollett demonstrated the difference in drift time by casting to identical pieces of water. Without the mend the drift was good, but brief and fishless. With the mend the drift was extended by perhaps eighteen inches, and just at the end a small rainbow of fifteen inches took. He had made his point.

This type of trout hunting is an acquired touch and feel (and, many anglers have said to me, an acquired taste in trout fishing that is not for them).

I like a 9'0", seven-weight rod, but others, including Tollett, who fishes the river over 100 days a year, prefer a 9'6". Weight forward and shooting tapers, coupled with leaders anywhere from seven to twelve feet, predominate around here. A 3X tippet is nice for feel, but a good fish will smoke this like it is a spider web. If you go larger than 3X, however, you lose contact with your flies beneath the surface and have trouble detecting strikes. This obviously is a Catch-22 situation, and the decision is partially subjective, one that an angler will make based on experience and preference. I'll stay with 3X for reasons of increased action and take my chances, relying on legendary angling skills (just ask Tollett) to land a big trout.

There is such an incredible fertility to the Beaverhead water that the multitudes of huge hatches must be experienced to be believed. A dry fly is often lost in the myriad, swirling insects. One evening we observed the mating flights of caddis so thick that they obscured both the bank and the water, but there was no sign of feeding trout on the surface. Once again nymphs caught fish when a dry fly seemed to be the only logical selection. The Beaverhead is maddening in this respect. What experience and observation tell you to do often results in wasted effort.

"I don't know, maybe they're feeding on emergers or they fed on them in the afternoon and are satiated now," commented Oswald. "With the exception of the crane flies, this is a very small community made up of caddis, smaller mayflies, and small stone flies."

And no one has yet formulated a direct correlation between stormy weather and fishing. "I see no rhyme or reason to it," said Oswald. "The weather makes or breaks you. One day I hid in the willows during a real goose drowner—thunder, lightning, wind, rain. In the two hours after this storm I had some of the best fishing ever. I suppose if somebody really studied this, they would figure it out, but I haven't yet."

So let's say you're going to take the Beaverhead seriously and devote a minimum of five long, hard days and evenings on the river. What are the best patterns for nymph fishing here? Tollett likes the Partridge & Peacock, LaFontaine Antrons, Red Squirrel Nymph, Hare's Ear, and Pheasant Tail for nonspecific conditions, such as when crane and stone flies are present. At these times he suggests T's Crane Nymph, Little Beaverhead Stone, and George's Brown Stone. Tollett also uses Flashback patterns that include Dark Olive Browns, Callibaetis, and Hare's Ears.

On another float, this time on a shifty October day, my good friend Tony Acerrano, guide Tim Mosolf, and I worked long and hard with just one five-pound, crazed rainbow to show for our efforts. But what a fish. Tim must have drifted a point fly (a nymph in this case) and dropper (an emerger) through this one run fifty times before the patterns worked right down the fish's feeding lane. Immediately his rod doubled over with stress and the rainbow arced well above the water three times, coming back to earth with a loud crashing and smacking as the guy headed for the pool below us with Tim in awkward pursuit. Several minutes later the trout came grudgingly to Tim and was netted by Tony. Big, strong, and solid, the fish powered back to deep water as soon as it was released.

Much later, after abandoning the nymphs in favor of a Woolly Bugger, a brown about the same size shot out sharklike from beneath an overhanging willow near a collapsing pasture fence and hit my offering as soon as it touched water. No leaping show of force here. The brown just turned sideways in the current and refused to move. I applied as much pressure as I thought the tippet would stand. All I received for my efforts was the sight of the brown twenty feet away flashing its body as it maintained its bite in the river. A couple of minutes of this silliness produced a standoff, but in that time Mosolf had worked us to a gravel bar, where I climbed out of the raft and slowly worked the fish to net. It was over two feet, more gold than brown, with vivid crimson and black spotting. A classic fall-run Beaverhead brown. That trout made my day, and I spent the rest of the float smoking good cigars, drinking lukewarm beer, and watching Tony and Tim fish. That's all it takes for me on this river: one good fish.

Whether this angling is for you is a matter of choice. The Beaverhead is a damn hard river to fish. It can be filled with frustration, but it is also an extremely challenging piece of water. Turning a big brown or a rainbow here is the reward for persistence and one of the most satisfying angling experiences I have ever stumbled into.

Gallatin River

*T*he Royal Coachman was taking an awful beating on that special day of my dimming past. If the pattern was actually a living thing, you would feel sorry for it, but since it was nothing more than a twisted melange of feathers and thread, there was no need for sympathy in this particular situation.

The experience exploded on one of those July afternoons that Montana travel brochures brag about. Temperatures in the eighties, a little bit of breeze pushing some white, fluffy cumulus clouds across the Gallatin Valley, and rainbow trout on every cast.

Drag-free floats. Bellied-up-in-the-current floats. Dragged-under-the-surface-and-drowned-like-a-rat floats. The fish couldn't care less; they were hitting anything that moved past their holding spots behind midstream boulders, tight against grassy banks, and out in the wide-open riffles. The Gallatin River here above its junction with the Taylor Fork was maybe fifty feet wide and could be waded if some caution were exercised. In the bright midday light you could see the trout holding steady all over, just above the colorful gravel and rock streambed. The rainbows averaged ten inches, and a couple of sprightly little devils hit the fourteen-inch mark, but size was not a consideration. Playing the energetic trout on a light cane rod, watching their miniature leaps, and feeling their determined runs across the current—that was more than enough and remains so to this day.

I'll never forget that outing, my first on a Montana trout stream. It was almost twenty-five years ago, and I was just a teenage Bozo from Illinois out in the "Wild West." I didn't know much of anything about the state, and this ignorance was not a point of concern in my young, naive existence.

My life was changed forever and for the better that day. I realized that although chasing girls and a good time was the main point of high school, casting flies to trout offered charms and a disarming honesty of a unique, uncompromising nature. Women's ways are still confusing, especially those of my wife and daughters, but the fascination with trout remains a full-blown curiosity. I understand that this is somewhat pathetic, but every time I think of the Gallatin I get a feeling in my stomach that reminds me of a crush I once had in sixth grade on a little blond sweetie. Talk about layered emotion.

This fly fishing business has proved itself to be weird, powerful stuff. And the Gallatin River's attraction is such that I manage to make the 600-mile-plus round trip from the state's northwest corner to the valley (south of Bozeman) at least once a year. And except when heavy rains have muddied the Taylor Fork and the water in the river below or when my timing is off and I hit the stream during spring runoff, the fishing is always as rewarding as on that first riotous afternoon.

To hell with Tom Wolfe and his sorry routine about not being able to go home again. Every time I see the river, step into it, and cast a line out over it, time vanishes and I'm a kid again. I'm free, with no worries and no responsibilities. No other river I've ever fished has the power to work this transformation so completely. After a day here, I have real trouble pulling myself back into accepted reality. No river has ever given me more.

Trout hunting on the Gallatin can be somewhat better than quite good, as one fish and game study of the late 1980s on a lower section of water indicated. There were almost 800 trout per mile over eleven inches, many of them rainbows of around one foot and a number of browns in the pounds region. I've heard reports suggesting that the browns may on very rare occasions exceed ten pounds and that there are over 100 brown trout per mile in the lower sections. In the water I'm familiar with, browns are fewer in number, but I've caught a few that weighed more than three pounds.

The Gallatin has a number of different stretches, but the ones I know a little bit about are from the Taylor Fork down to Big Sky and from the Taylor Fork twisting up into the river's mountainous headwaters in Yellowstone National Park (some refer to this portion as the West Gallatin River, an unnecessary affectation that will not be acknowledged here). There's good water—the big brown trout type—below these two sections, and sometimes a landowner will let a person fish the river below Gallatin Canyon and not too far from scenic, uptown Bozeman. The parts I like, though more remote, are accessible to the common man from either road or trail.

Fishing this water has the virtues of simplicity and/or complexity, with the choice up to the angler and his level of trouting skill and personal preference on any given day. If you want to take things easy, tie on a dry line like the Coachman and work the obvious pocket water and riffles. If you are in an aggressive mood and feel up to some challenging work, put on a short, stout leader at the end of a full-tilt, quick-sinking line and a large nymph like Charles Brooks's Assam Dragon and probe the depths of some racy, deep run. Hard work often pays off in big, hard fish. The choice is yours.

When I started fishing the river I always went the first route. It was just a blast being able to catch a bunch of rainbows on dries with no more complications than finding a place to pull off U.S. Highway 191 and rig up. After chasing the noble carp (a species I truly do respect, but that's the makings of another fantasy) for so many years in the warm, turbid, and very polluted waters of southern Wisconsin, tying into trout with such ease was something too pleasant to resist.

But times have changed. Ten years back, 90 percent of my fishing was with dries, but today that 90 percent is spent beneath the water's

The Gallatin River in late October.

surface manipulating, sometimes with the illusion of competency, nymphs, streamers, and wet fly patterns. This nonpurist transformation began when I first read Charles Brooks's *Nymph Fishing for Larger Trout*. This approach opened the door to a new range of unrealistic expectations. Being fooled by twelve-inch fish is a source of endless fascination, but there are times when measuring successful disappointments in increments of pounds rather than inches offers curious and fulfilling amusement. Many fly fishers who are extremely skilled with the dry fly scornfully refer to these methods as bait fishing. I find that unless the conditions are just right—dumb fish, obvious hatch, easy-to-read current—I rarely take many large trout on dries anymore. On the other hand, with nymphs I consistently catch trout over two pounds. I like touching fish that have a size and heft to them that is not commonly associated with their twelve-inch brethren. So much for salmonid polemics.

There is a nice, glassy run right by the highway and just up from the Taylor's Fork that always holds some entertaining rainbows. To fish this piece of turf properly you must cross well above it so that you cast into the water from just short of midstream. There are slightly frightening overtones attendant with this location, especially in the gathering gloom of dusk, as you are standing in fast water well over your knees right next to very fast water over your shoulders. Fall here and you'll stay wet for a long time.

With a six- or seven-weight sinking line, a four- or five-foot leader tapering to a delicate leader in 1X or 0X, the Assam Dragon #4 or Montana Stone #2, a lead twist-on or two (extremely delicate angling is going on here), and a nine-foot rod, the angler begins his exploration of the arcane. Actually this is not as awkward or difficult as it may seem, and the technique works very well on all similar water in the Gallatin and throughout Montana. Semi-master (that's as far as I've progressed) this routine and you'll take big fish on any river.

Starting at the head of the run, cast the contraption about twenty feet upstream, allowing it to sink to the bottom, and work right through the run. Keep the slightest bit of slack in the line, but not so much that you can't feel, see, and sense (this comes rapidly with experience) the nymph bouncing along the gravel and rounded rocks of the streambed. This is where the trout are holding in the benthic or slower water that is created by the' size of the obstructions and the drag of the bottom. It is the only place that is calorically efficient for big trout to hold. Anywhere else and the energy expended to maintain a holding position in the current would outweigh any potential gain from a stream of aquatic insects whizzing by.

Many so-called authorities adamantly suggest that you strike at any deviance in the movement of the nymph through its down-deep journey. I disagree. When a good trout hits it will be a vicious strike as the fish zips up after the food and then powers straight back to cover. You'll know when it happens. The rod tip will often be jerked into the water. Sure, a few fish are missed, but many more are taken simply because each cast is fished more thoroughly.

At the end of the drift, allow the fly to swing in the current for a few seconds, the time needed to take out the belly that accumulated in the cast as it was fighting the many conflicting currents in the water column. On occasion a big boy will hammer the fly at this time, an enlightening experience that normally comes while I'm staring at a rock cliff or off into space with out-of-focus visions of the golden age of the Woodstock generation staggering through my head.

If you are right-handed and the current is moving from left to right, making the next cast is not difficult. Just strip in the line with your left hand and lift the rod simultaneously with your right. Flip the works back upstream. It will look a little like attempting a hook shot in basketball. Basically, you are making a single haul of short dimensions.

When the current is moving from right to left, each cast is a reverse effort and made backhand, which would seem to be more difficult but is not. With a little practice, the cast can be made with consistent accuracy. The only difference seems to be that the nymph tends to land a little farther out and away from you.

Brooks suggests repeating this move many times, but a half-dozen efforts is my limit before lengthening the cast a few feet and repeating the procedure. After thirty-five feet of line is out, things take on dangerous overtones with lead and hooks flying all over the place, frequently into the back of my head. Time to move downstream a couple of yards and try again.

The first fish I took here using this method was on the Dragon and was just short of two feet. It was my first BIG trout. Up to that moment I had had little confidence in Brooks's teachings because I had taken only a fish or two—which I attributed to persistence and a casual conjunction with good fortune (qualities I've learned that most good fly fishers have in abundance). Right in the middle of the hundredth drift of the day, the line stopped dead in a current that was well over ten miles an hour. Convinced I was hung up on the bottom I yanked hard in an upward direction. The line razored upstream instantly, cutting through the dark green water, and seconds later a very large, upset rainbow rocketed above the surface heading for the moon. The sound that that fish made when it smacked back into the water was a big fish noise. No other words describe the sensation. When you hear the energy and power of that sound you're addicted. It's like lusting (well, maybe just hoping) for the scream of a reel as line disappears on a big run.

There were three more leaps and crashes and then a serious session holding dead still at the bottom just above the run. Fearing for the tippet's life, I gave the fish gentle treatment, but holding in the fast water tired him. After one quick burst upstream, without leaping, he was led to the net.

A friend of mine once observed that whenever a good trout is close at hand everyone says "Nice fish!" He's right, and I'm afraid that's all I could think to say to this specimen. "Nice fish!" That is what nymphing on the Gallatin can do for a person: put him into sizeable trout with a fair degree of consistency.

Some years ago when I still believed that backpacking possessed some redeeming values, a couple of friends and I strolled up the drainage to Gallatin Lake, which rests quietly at 8,834 feet. We got a late start and managed only three or four miles upstream, but we didn't care as we passed through splendid green hills of native grasses and sagebrush. Pine forest wandered up and away on all sides. Here and there in likely looking pools we cast Royal Wulffs and Adamses and took small rainbows of about eight inches. Enough, maybe six or seven, were kept for dinner.

We set up camp in a grassy meadow near a copse of aspen perhaps 100 yards from the river, which ran smoothly through this gentle stage of the valley. The Gallatin was not more than twenty-five feet wide here, and two of us took a couple more trout for sport while our companion, who liked to cook, started a small fire of downed and dry aspen twigs and sticks. (This was back when you were still supposed to be having a good time out in the country and a slightly smoking, crackling fire was an integral part of that scenario. I have had a gas stove for nearly twenty years that I've never used. When I camp I build a fire of wood or have a cold camp.)

At any rate, when we returned to camp, dinner was ready. The trout, mushroom soup, and fried potatoes tasted great. The evening was calm and the light was taking on an orange glow as we all just relaxed to our own rhythms and incoherencies—that is, until a large bull moose appeared with the obvious intention of passing directly through our campsite to the river to dine graciously on green grasses and sip delicately of the pure waters found there.

We'd made an error in location, and the moose, a species that has caused me more trouble than any grizzly, snorted and appeared ready to kill us. There was not a lot we could do, so we ran like hell into the trees, which proved to be a wise decision. The animal's rack was too wide to permit him access to our sanctuary. The moose went on down to the Gallatin and ate his fill. The sight of him slurping the grass and water while standing in the stream is still clear in my mind.

His repast took about two months, and then he came back through camp, stopping to look us over with alien appraisal (actually we were the foreigners here) before disappearing over a distant hill. We did not sleep well that night and were up and on the trail before dawn.

The path took us through dark forest and then across a meadow covered with wildflowers in reds, blues, whites, and yellows. A small herd of elk spotted us and bounded quickly away into the pines. We stopped for lunch. I set out on a brief walk that ended abruptly when I saw recent bear tracks in a snowbank and mud. The ones in the mud were much wider than my extended fingers and still filling with water. After informing my companions of this gentle discovery, we did what we normally do in situations bordering on complicated—we panicked and scrambled up the trail as fast as we could for as long as we could, pans, bottles, and cans of fruit cocktail clanging away in the mountain air. Two hundred yards later, nearly dead from the effort, we collapsed by the Gallatin River, now turned mountain stream. We were thirsty, and the ice-cold water tasted good. Our fear added some spice to the adventure. The bear failed to make an appearance.

Several hours of hiking brought us to open parkland beneath wild, snow-covered peaks. According to our map, Gallatin Lake was just half a mile ahead. And from what the honest-looking person at the fly shop in West Yellowstone had told us, every cast should yield a monster trout. Suspicion was already growing, because this person had also informed us that the trip into the lake was only an hour's walk that he and his family, including two toddlers, made each Sunday. We'd already invested five hours, but we figured that being out of shape and carrying heavy backpacks were adding to our journey's length.

The next day we started off with our rods but were soon slogging through waste-deep snow as a warm July sun baked our brains. Two hours later we were at the lake. It was very pretty, but we could see that the fishing was going to be somewhat difficult. Gallatin Lake was frozen solid. We'd been had by a fun-loving West Yellowstone local. The three of us had invested more time, effort, and money on fruitless endeavors in the past, however, so we were not upset—which could not be said for the person in the fly shop when we returned and dragged him halfway across a glass display case offering severely over-priced fly reels. He threatened to call the cops so we left town without even visiting Dinosaur Land or buying any Montana copper jewelry.

A couple of winters ago, while browsing through Steve Pierce's informative book, *The Lakes of Yellowstone,* I learned that Gallatin Lake was 19.5 acres with a maximum depth of forty-seven feet and was fishless. There are some very funny people in West Yellowstone, I guess.

Several times recently I've fished the meandering, somewhat wild-looking portions of the river that are accessible from the highway, as well as the lower parts we encountered on the ill-fated hike. I have always taken a number of rainbows (and a few whitefish) on dries and nymphs. Never has a fish been bigger than fourteen inches, but the effort has always been rewarding: relatively easy fishing in very nice country.

Some years back, when my family and I (they let me travel with them in odd-numbered years) were staying at a local dude ranch in the valley, my stepbrother and I fished under the guidance of an individual named Yellowstone Jack. The guy knew the water and knew how to take trout, but he was not prepared to deal with a sibling rivalry that has spanned decades and is at once timeless.

Yellowstone Jack helped us rig up and sent us on our way upstream at different points along the Gallatin. The fishing was good, and my stepbrother and I began catching rainbows immediately and with regularity, and we both became keyed into how the other was doing. This soon degenerated into tag-team fly fishing, with rapid casts to each piece of holding water, a quick set of the hook, and even quicker sliding of the hapless trout to eager fingers for a quick release. Then it was on again up to the next hole splashing and crashing as, I'm sure, frightened hordes of salmonids fled for their very lives before our mad charges.

This activity continued for a couple of hours (and no doubt rendered that stretch of the river worthless for several weeks). Returning to the beginning, we found Yellowstone Jack sitting on the tailgate of the pickup truck. I think "sardonic" aptly describes his facial set and attitude.

"You fellers fish like that back east?"

"What do you mean?" we replied, more or less trying to feign ignorance of our obviously boorish behavior.

"Let me phrase things this way," said Yellowstone Jack slowly. "That was the biggest load of bullshit I've ever seen on a river around here and I've seen a lot of it in my time."

Well, we felt pretty sorry after that, and ever since I've tried to behave myself on a trout stream. Yellowstone Jack's scorn was perhaps the best lesson (and the toughest to accept) I've learned on the Gallatin.

My fishing here pretty much mirrors my experiences elsewhere. There have been successes, fine times, mistakes, and slight humiliations. A steady learning curve that has applied to more than chasing trout.

The river is always changing, and each visit has its own unique set of variables. Once in November when the sky cleared and the temperature hit the seventies there were whitefish everywhere and not a rainbow to be found. It was a day when the water was moving perfectly clear and blue across the colorful rocks and I started believing that maybe this would be the one all-time magic year when winter would never come . . . and I knew all the time that the feeling was just good old-fashioned Gallatin River voodoo. And that, of course, was why I was there in the first place.

Bighorn River

*I*magine a fertile river loaded with aquatic plant and animal life flourishing in cold, clear water. The river drifts easily through a gentle valley in the wide-open plains country way out West. A large mountain range rolling away into Wyoming adds to the spectacle. And, yes, there are good numbers of healthy trout here. Fish that willingly take a fly. Browns and rainbows weighing a few pounds and sometimes more.

Maybe the river happens to be the Bighorn. If this is the case, consider that no stream in Montana has received more attention from the outdoor media than this one winding through the Crow Indian Reservation in the south-central region of the state.

Ever since the water below the Yellowtail Dam was opened to fishing in the sixties, angling writers have raved about the trophy browns and rainbows that are taken on a regular basis. When you have a river holding more than twice as many fish exceeding twelve inches in each mile than the world-famous Madison, this attention is not all that difficult to understand. All of us with the trout-fishing fever running through our fragile veins dream of waters like the Bighorn. With an average flow of 3,000 cubic feet per second making wading a sporting proposition, taking to the sea in ships is a convenient and safe alternative, so the large numbers of people floating the river is understandable.

This publicity has translated into incredible fishing pressure on the first thirteen-mile stretch of water known as the Upper 13. On a pleasant summer day you will encounter literally hundreds of anglers fishing from shore and a greater number working the river from drift boats and rafts. Can gridlock on the Bighorn be far away?

Verbal confrontations and even fights have resulted from this heavy traffic. For example, one bright September day some friends and I floated the river. We got our normal late-morning start, and the river was already jammed with boats and wading anglers. Jockeying for position on prime stretches was common, and we saw some turf battles during the bizarre adventure. Oars flashed in the sun as boats, stacked like arriving jets over La Guardia, maneuvered for position in prime holding water. Those with fish already on tried valiantly to keep their trout from being broken off or run over by other boats and rafts. They were not always successful, and these failures were often punctuated with creative strings of expletives. Happy anglers were swearing at one another, throwing rocks in the water, and, in general, just having a whale of a fine time under the Big Sky.

The whole mad situation reminded me of the 1968 Democratic Convention in Chicago. The behavior of the fly fishers involved in this travesty made about as much sense as that political fiasco.

Yet even under these adverse conditions, our party took a number of browns and rainbows in the eighteen- to twenty-inch range. And this was on a crystal-clear, bluebird-weather day that was anything but ideal for fishing. The rainbows leaped high in the air and the browns made fierce, deep runs. Classic stuff we fly fishers live for.

Just ten years ago the fishing here was unbelievable (obviously in some respects it still is), but once the word really hit the streets about how damn good the angling can be at times, the number of angler days on the river skyrocketed and the size and numbers of trout began to decrease.

What is even more distressing is that a very small number of very vocal guides and outfitters who make good money from the Bighorn fail to recognize the seriousness of the problem or are unwilling to risk a single dollar of their guiding fees to change the situation. They insist that very big trout in good numbers are being caught by most anglers every day of the year. Their cacophony drowns out the voices of those who have the river's best interests at heart. It is possible that in the near future there will have to be some type of registration system or limitation on the numbers of people allowed to fish the Bighorn on any given day, or the trout will suffer and a quality angling experience will no longer exist.

Some of us look for other things when we are on a river, like a quiet time, the peace and tranquillity of just drifting with the current, and good fellowship. What we are not after is aggression, frustration, anger, and trout with ripped mouths, torn gill covers, ragged fins, and missing eyes. We're willing to sacrifice unlimited access on rivers like the Bighorn in order to preserve the aesthetics of fly fishing.

So does all of this mean that an angler should avoid the Bighorn entirely? The answer is "No." And there are some things you can do to improve the odds for a pleasant and successful day adrift. For people who have little fly fishing experience or have never taken a good trout, the Bighorn is a nice place to start.

Many of the articles I've read on fishing this river claim that fish are taken by the dozens, quite a few in the five-pound and up range. Tales of ninety-fish days with trout averaging three pounds or more abound. Times like these do occur every year in surprising numbers, but my experience, and the experiences of anglers whose judgment I trust, indicates something more modest for most of us most of the time. But even these diminished expectations are quite optimistic. A person who fishes hard, who works with diligence at his angling, will probably take a half-dozen or more trout that should average around sixteen inches in a day's fishing. Most of us can live within these parameters.

Experienced and/or lucky anglers have a legitimate chance to connect with one of the big boys, but to come to this water and expect a

The author with a Bighorn rainbow.

tackle-busting fight on every cast is extremely unrealistic. It is an attitude destined for disappointment.

In addition to the Upper 13, there are two other stretches of water of similar length: from Bighorn to Mallard and from Mallard to Two-Leggins. Working these places will help you avoid much of the madding crowd, but, as with most solutions, there are some trade-offs. Chief among the disadvantages are low water and water quality problems caused by poor irrigation practices in the valley. This is most often the case for the lower portion of these stretches from Rotten Grass on. In addition, access is difficult in spots. Many of the outfitters prefer not to float this water. The consensus is that these two lower stretches have fewer but larger fish, and they receive less angling pressure.

"I've never taken anyone down that part of the river who hasn't caught at least a few fish," said outfitter David Schaff of nearby

Hardin. "There are some water quality problems, but you can still catch fish."

Now that you are completely discouraged and saying to yourself that the Bighorn is out of the question, read on. Mixed in with the negative information is a healthy dose of positive news.

If you wish to fish the Upper 13 from shore, from a rental boat, or with a guide (see the list in the Notes and Comments section), hit the water by 8:00 A.M. This will put you on the river before the bulk of the neoprene-clad armada sets sail. You'll be fishing over trout that have not been sensitized (or traumatized) by the offerings of several anglers before you, and you will have a much more peaceful experience floating a very pretty river in relatively serene surroundings. As summer gives way to fall, the number of fly fishers declines slightly, and there is a subtle shift to more dedicated individuals whose main interest is jumping large fish. They are here hunting big browns and rainbows. Gone are many of the summertime crazies more intent on chugging vast quantities of beer while foul-hooking their guide with errant casts.

A nine-foot rod with a six- or seven-weight line will handle all of the water. You want a rod that is light enough to make casting a fun challenge, but not so dainty that it lacks the backbone to deal with a stout breeze or to pressure a strong fish using the current to increase its fighting advantage. A longer rod will also allow you to extend the float of your fly, nymph, or streamer. The added length will allow you to keep the line off the water to some degree and avoid the swirling currents and eddies that add drag to the drift and spook the trout.

There is a little bit of everything on the river—long, deep, glassy runs; deep holes; riffles; undercut banks; submerged logs; feeding lanes between clumps of aquatic plants—all flowing down a relatively sedate gradient that gives you time to place your casts.

Choosing the proper pattern here can be as complicated as you wish, but a few basic flies will take fish on most of the river most of the time. These include Blue-Winged Olives #16–20, Pale Morning

Duns #18–20, Black Caddis #16–18, Tan Caddis #14–18, Yellow Stone Fly #10–14, and Midges #18–22.

The following very basic listing of hatches gives an approximate time frame for using the flies just mentioned: blue-winged olives from April through May and from mid-September through mid-December, pale morning duns from mid-July through late August, yellow stone flies from mid-July through early September, black caddis from mid-August through mid-October, tan caddis from mid-August into early October, and tricos starting in mid-August and lasting to mid-October.

Because of the relatively small size of these patterns you will want to use at least nine-foot leaders (twelve would be better) tapered down to 4X, 5X, and even 6X. These very fine tippets will help you fool the fish, but the trade-off is that a good fish will break you off more often than not. The decision is yours. I prefer the smaller tippets and increased action despite the frustration of lost fish. Lost opportunities are part of the sport's romance and charm, anyway.

If you want or need to use nymphs, tying on any of the following should work: Brassie #14–16, gold-ribbed Hare's Ear #12–16, yellow-gold Scud #8–12, or Pheasant Tail #14–18. These need to be fished right along the bottom, and a twist-on or two of lead will sink them down where they can do their best work. Sink-tip lines are, for the most part, difficult to fish and unnecessary if you use some lead on a leader that is no more than $7\frac{1}{2}$ feet long, preferably less, and maybe 2X or 3X tippet. You need to stay in touch with the nymph (a familiar but vital axiom), allowing it to roll along the bottom while still maintaining sufficient contact slightly short of a tight line. You can also fish these with a dropper setup, with the nymph on the point and maybe an emerger or wet fly on the tag end.

As for streamers, all in the #2–6 range, the usual gang that includes Woolly Buggers, Zonkers, Muddler Minnows, and Spruce Flies will get the attention of big trout. Cast these bank tight or even on the bank, in front of and behind midstream boulders and along sweepers and logjams, and then immediately begin to strip them back toward you.

When a fish hits a streamer fished this way, you'll know it. The same leader you used for nymphing works well here.

One last pattern that may be the best fish taker in the bunch is also the most controversial. I am referring to the infamous San Juan Worm. This thing imitates the red worms found in the river-bottom detritus. All trout, especially the big ones, love to munch on these worms, but a fairly large puritanical segment of the fly fishing population abhors the use of the San Juan Worm. I can tell you with absolute confidence that this pattern will catch fish on the Bighorn at all times. And I find the use of this pattern no more offensive than using a day-glo red-egg pattern for Alaskan salmon or the latest craze, fish-flesh flies. After all, when you get down to basics, every fly pattern imitates some sort of fauna's flesh in some state or another. The choice is yours. For me, living the life of a purist is a futile and hypocritical pursuit.

Because you will find trout holding throughout the river, long casts are not necessary. With practice, any caster can make good casts at this range and take plenty of trout in the process. One day I watched an extremely skilled angler take several good fish from a feeding pod. Not one of his casts was more than thirty-five feet, but each offering was made with pinpoint accuracy and extreme delicacy. When he hooked a trout, the fish was immediately and quietly worked away from the others still feeding, played, and then released. All of this took place while he was sitting on the bow of his beached raft. It was a very nice exhibition of precision, patience, and craft.

When you do connect with a trout, get the fish on the reel as quickly as possible. By this I mean either wind any slack back onto your reel or carefully let the line run out through your line hand as the fish makes its first run. You will have much more control over the situation when you can play the fish from the reel. On crowded days, you will need every advantage you can get. Boats and rafts will be roaming all over the place, and at times you will need to guide your trout away from heavy traffic.

The power of this river affects even those who claim to have little interest in fly fishing. People who have kicked the fly fishing habit for years can become addicted again when they experience the Bighorn. For example, some friends and I, needing a break from early-season grouse hunting, decided to float the river one day. One of our group protested loudly (but good naturedly) that fishing, particularly for trout, possessed no redeeming values that he could divine. This individual went on to state that in his "misguided youth" he had spent some time fishing for trout but had eventually seen the light and now spent all of his time hunting upland birds with a shotgun (in fact, he was actually something of a recognized authority on quality or "best" guns, but we were willing to overlook this obvious character defect).

The first hour of our float was fishless, but then a rainbow of sizeable proportions struck a nymph being dragged through a deep pocket and executed a series of leaps, runs, and splashes. The fish waged a serious battle, aided by the river's current. Even with a strong rod, turning the trout was difficult. On the edges of my vision I noticed that our shotgunning expert was leaning over from his seat in the bow to observe the action and the rainbow, which was well over twenty inches of bright silver.

Several minutes later, I tied into a good brown along a current seam next to a riffle. The fish ran swiftly for some time before being brought to net. This brightly colored fish of over twenty inches also attracted the interest of our bird-hunting devotee.

We had packed spare waders, boots, and a rod in case this person decided to fish. I noticed that he was casting away in a deep run while the rest of us finished lunch on shore. He was now clad in waders and was intent on his fishing. The rest of the day he fished with zeal and a certain degree of skill, taking several browns over twenty inches. In fact, he out-fished all of us. A sandbagger was in our midst, and that was fine with us.

On the ride back to the motel his talk was strictly of the fishing and how he "could see where there might be some sport in casting for big trout on a river like the Bighorn." He wanted to know the cost and other details of the rod and reel he had used. Obviously he was hooked, and the Bighorn and its trout were to blame. Current rumor is that he now carries a travel rod on all of his bird-hunting forays. Another decent soul lies ruined out on the Montana dreamscape.

Despite the crowds, there is a compelling nature to the Bighorn. You know there are lots of decent fish in the river and that with a modicum of effort you will catch several during the day. One August evening, as dusk and the following darkness closed in, caddis rose from the water in numbers sufficient to excite the trout, but not in clouds that would have made fishing a function of blind luck. (When there are millions of insects hatching, having a trout select your offering from among the masses is a long shot. Prolific hatches are a wonder to watch, but they are also a bitch to fish on most occasions.) The three of us would float for a while, then anchor and cast dries above channels between beds of green growth that gently waved back and forth in the current. Trout came up immediately and hit our flies on every cast. Sometimes the fly was attacked the moment its hackles touched the water.

Bankside glides, runs along downed trees, riffles, and eddies offered the same extravagant trout banquet. We fished until we had our fill of action and pulled up to the takeout after midnight. The Milky Way was a glowing band of silver-white, and there was just the faintest suggestion of movement in the air. Coyotes talked back and forth in the night, communicating a wild nighttime joy.

After the boat was loaded and gear stowed, we lingered by the river, unwilling to end things. This had been one of the rare ones, a day with few boats and plenty of trout. A Bighorn special—the kind that ensures your return.

Musselshell River

$\mathcal{D}$on't expect to be treated like royalty when you visit the Musselshell valley in central Montana. The most prolific population of fence posts with orange spray-painted tops (indicating No Trespassing) in North America resides in the wide-open sage flats, pastures, fields, and foothills. And there must be at least 25,000 signs proclaiming "No Hunting, No Fishing, and No Trespassing" nailed to anything standing over three feet above the ground. How an individual can practice the first two activities without engaging in the third is something of a perplexity, but never mind that. The fact remains that there are some very pretty brown trout swimming in the Musselshell River.

Fortunately for those of us not accorded the privilege of being landed gentry in this expansive valley, the local citizenry slipped up sometime in the past and allowed the state of Montana to acquire a public access site that rests along one of the most productive stretches of water. A sign on the south side of U.S. 12 near Martinsdale indicates Selkirk Fishing Access Site. There are some sizeable trout hanging around this stretch of the river.

After the spring runoff and before the Musselshell is drawn down from irrigation, the river here is classic big brown water, bending and curving through open country with untold numbers of holding areas beneath the grassy and brushy banks. Water spills over sand and gravel shelves into deep pools shaded from the persistent sun by alders and cottonwoods. Riffles and silent glides swing lazily in soft arcs as the stream moves gently toward its rendezvous with the Missouri at Fort Peck Reservoir 150 miles to the northeast.

You can camp at the access (though not for more than two weeks straight, according to another sign), and there are the usual sumptuous amenities, including picnic tables carefully notched with salient points concerning the love lives of visiting dignitaries. There are also outhouses for the secretive among us. Large mosquitoes in big numbers call this place home. Local Mountain, Bald Ridge, and the rest of the Crazies are visible in the south and the Castle range rises in the west.

The Musselshell runs for well over 200 miles, but the stretch below Martinsdale, beginning with the confluence of the North and South forks and down to Harlowton, is where the trout fisher must concentrate his efforts. This section is perhaps 25 miles long, but the water available at Selkirk is considerably less than that. All the same, thoroughly working what is available takes a few days. The population is mostly brown trout in decent but not Bighorn River numbers, with far fewer rainbows and brookies. Herds of marauding whitefish are a common spectacle.

In other words, the Musselshell is not a destination river for those who must travel long distances to reach its banks. Rather, this is a place to fish on the way to locations like Yellowstone or the Missouri River or Glacier National Park up by the Canadian border.

The river is easy to wade—not deep and rarely exceeding twenty feet wide—and your entrance is best planned well ahead by cautiously approaching the water to consider the tactical and logistical problems ahead. Usually by late June things have settled down so that some of the browns are visible holding along the bottom or when they make brief rushes out into the open to take a nymph or an unwary minnow.

There are no crowds here, but the trout are spooky, perhaps from the many hawks riding the thermals far above. Quiet, low-profile movements are in order. The Musselshell is perfect for a two- or three-weight rod and a nine-foot (or longer) leader tapered to, at the absolute maximum, 3X, with 4X or 5X preferred.

One summer my enthusiasm got the better of what passes for self-control. After setting up camp I went fishing, even though the sun was directly overhead. After scouting the water, executing a delicate entry, and maneuvering into casting position, I rifled an extraordinary effort of perhaps thirty-two feet that quartered upstream, landing with only marginal disturbance next to the bank. The weighted Hare's Ear Nymph (creative solutions to angling problems were in full bloom that afternoon) dropped quickly through the current and was soon happily bouncing along the bottom. The run was shallow, perhaps three feet, and the water was clear, so the imitation's progress was easily determined.

With amazing swiftness, a trout swooped out from what I thought was just shadowed bank but was obviously a submerged shelter and gulped the nymph, the whiteness of its mouth flashing against the dark brown of the streambed. By setting the hook and drawing the line taut, I halted the brown's homeward return and upset him a bit as he streaked up from the bottom and wriggled across a shallow run, fin and back exposed to the warm air, into some deeper stuff just below a collection of stumps, limbs, and barbed wire. A rusting green and white 4-H sign was embedded in the tangled mess.

Two-weight rods are wonderfully delicate instruments to cast, but their strength is not impressive to any trout of size and distinction. I could hold the brown, sort of, and get back onto the reel, but that was the extent of my progress for several minutes. The situation took on humorous overtones much like Mark Twain telling the same bad joke over and over again to an audience that eventually laughed at the audacity and absurdity of the concept. The trout sulked and turned sideways in the mild bottom flow. I held court slightly downstream, rod arched beautifully, all the while concerned for the well-being of the slender tippet. "Never give an inch" was the operative phrase in this instance.

The Musselshell River in July near the Selkirk Access.

Five minutes spent like this is a long time, a near eternity that would probably be dragging on to this day, except that the trout possessed a somewhat smaller brain than I did and no doubt was becoming concerned and frustrated with his stalemated circumstance. He moved upstream to harsher water. It quickly became apparent that maintaining the previous position had been difficult labor. One brief dash into the wall of current finished the trout and he came swiftly to net. This had proved to be an uneventful struggle from the perspective of acrobatics and steelhead-like runs, but I'd never been connected to a stationary trout for so long in moving water.

Many fly fishers scorn browns, but I find them to be great fish: muscular, streamlined, crafty, and beautifully marked like this one. The black and scattered crimson spots spread along the creature's brown, steel, and golden flanks shone in the hard light. The power of the fish returned as it caught its breath in the tranquil eddy where I was standing. A slight release of my hold on the caudal peduncle was sufficient for the brown to escape and submarine directly back to its cave.

Enough for an afternoon. It was time to enjoy the day, the view, and one or two cold beers. Midway through a very fine cigar (Costa Rican, Cameroon wrapper), my thoughts returned to a trip here earlier this spring that underscored the singular unfriendliness, or maybe the poorly understood strangeness, of the Musselshell valley and its inhabitants (anomalous behavior in a state known for friendly natives).

After spending several hours fighting a heavy early-May snowstorm and the creative driving the weather spawned, I saw the Selkirk sign and set up camp. My cursory examination of the river revealed high and off-color conditions, but some serious weighted-streamer action produced a few browns and a small rainbow before I returned to camp and an evening's cup of coffee.

After enough years of weird behavior and lunatic events, a person's radar should be tuned to the level at which certain forms of human endeavor trigger ancient warning signals that what is happening now is some sort of benign metaphor for future badness. Such was not the case on this pleasant spring outing.

From out of nowhere, like a carnival conjuring act, an old fellow lurched and staggered past me humming an unrecognizable tune. The gentleman was wearing gray dress pants, black wingtips, a white shirt, a black tie, and a beret. A small beagle staggered along behind him. I figured, "What the hell? This is Montana."

"How's it goin'?" I asked.

"I'm walking the dog." Lurch, shuffle, and stagger.

"Sure is a nice night."

"The dog needs to walk at night." And the soft dance continued.

"Take care."

"Where's my dog?"

"Behind you there."

"Oh!"

The pair trundled off into the darkness and I climbed into my sleeping bag.

The next morning, after some orange juice and coffee, I marched off to the river, which was now a touch lower and clearer. An olive Woolly Bugger (more angling creativity) blasted bank tight, as is the pattern's only true destiny, brought regular and sprightly responses from brown trout running from fourteen inches up to eighteen. Fat, colorful fish, every one. The day was warm and sunny. It was just plain nice and easy fishing, the kind I like best most of the time. Last night's strangeness was not forgotten, but neither was it influencing my mood.

After a couple of hours of pleasant work that seemed to last minutes, I walked out of the water and down a dirt lane back to my tent. Red-winged blackbirds trilled electrically from branches overhead. The scene at my campsite was so much changed that I was unable to figure out what was different. The truck was still parked where I had left it. My cooler and cooking stuff were still scattered across the picnic table. And the grass over there was still matted from the tent.

The tent! Where in the hell was the tent?

The hair on my neck raised as from static electricity. I instinctively crouched down and whirled in a quick circle of reconnaissance. There was no one in sight, no sound, nothing. My tent, clothes, boots, sleeping bag, and a bunch of other stuff had vanished. There were no tire tracks, no footprints, and no tent stakes. My gear was in another time zone somewhere, and the day was not seriously confused, yet.

Reacting instinctively again, I grabbed a cold beer and downed it quickly. Then another. Twenty minutes of searching revealed nothing. Not a clue. Time to throw the cooler and cooking crate in the truck and head down the lonesome highway, which I did, in a hurry.

I was sure I was okay as far as where I had pitched my tent. All of the official-looking signs said so. No one else was staying at the access. I was a victim of some more Musselshell friendliness; that seemed to be the only answer. After several miles, anger replaced fear. I decided the time was ripe for some serious trespassing in "offlimitsville." I would even the score and take some of the locals' private stash of trout.

Over by the town of Lennep, past the rundown wooden buildings, and around the bend from the well-manicured , white-painted schoolhouse is a small creek that races and gurgles through a downscale draw. Parking well past the first orange-painted posts I could find, I rigged my two-weight like a man possessed, like a warrior on a sacred mission (viewed from a distance of several hundred miles and days, the event takes on epic overtones). No waders, no vest, no deet. This was man's sport.

For over three hours I worked that small stream like a crazed tenant farmer driving his only mule down a bone-dry field in a vain attempt to get some sort of crop in the ground. Neither of us had the slightest hope of success or of even marginal redemption as a result of our labors, but we were driven beasts. The anger and frustration must be assuaged.

Dozens of trout were taken, and not all of them were released. I kept enough for an angry banquet of excess over a fire that would rage in some other part of Montana. Revenge is mine, sayeth the madman clutching the fly rod. My multiple personalities voiced themselves amid whizzing weight-forward flylines. The three individuals looking down on me from a barren hill in the near distance wore curious, puzzled expressions.

Climbing out of the water and walking back to the truck beneath the silent gaze of those people felt right in a brain-damaged way. They said nothing, but I could hear their boots working the dust and stone above. They were still watching, I observed in the reflection of my side mirror, when I drove away toward the highway.

The beer tasted cold and yeasty in the dimness of the Mint Bar in Martinsdale. The bartender was unimpressed with my tale of the theft and suggested I contact the authorities in Harlowton. I decided against that since I'd already been there a few times in the past and no one I had observed around town seemed very happy or helpful. A couple of boys a few stools away thought the whole chain of events was funny and said so.

"Ripped off all of your shit, did they." This was not a question.

"Damn straight." I was still in an uproar.

"Sure as shit showed 'em, catching all them damn trout." They were really laughing now.

"Yah. I live 'round here and I'm pissed off," said the other between noises that actually sounded like "guffaws." Even the bartender and an oldtimer at the end of the bar were cracking up. After another beer the humor hit me like it was supposed to in Mark Twain's routine that I mentioned earlier, but even at this point I was not sure what was humorous.

Hell, the thieves had not gotten my fishing gear or cameras. I was not hurt. The stuff was insured. The truck still ran. I still had some money and some time to fish some more. And there were those traumatized trout hiding in that little creek. Perhaps the Musselshellville crew looked at things with a perspective that varied wildly from mine.

Even today thoughts of that trip occasionally produce some anger, and I'm more cautious, especially when I'm on the road alone. But at the time the surrounding hills were radiating an early evening glow, signaling post time. I put out my cigar and finished the beer. . . .

My experiences over the years on the Musselshell have an elliptical quality to them. In spite of serious efforts at exploration, gaps in my conception of a total experience with the river pop up with regularity. Yet my feelings toward the river are complete and satisfying (including the theft and the posted land).

I've caught and released as many good brown trout here as I have on any river I've fished, considering the amount of time invested. I've spent cold nights camping on national forest land along the headwaters of the Musselshell. I've cast all kinds of ugly patterns in the swiftly moving, gray-blue water down by Shamut, Ryegate, and Lavina in futile attempts to catch smallmouth bass that are rumored to be swimming in that portion of the stream. I've even spent some time talking with a few people who were using stink bait to catch catfish in the Musselshell up by Mosby on my way to Jordan and the Hell Creek region of the Charles M. Russell National Wildlife Refuge.

Still, even with all of these varied and entertaining incidents, my gut feeling is that I understand very little about the river. I know there are miles of uncharted water rolling along out there that I know nothing about. There could be monster browns cruising in those hidden niches of possible angling bliss. Wild beasts, maybe fearsome badgers or loathsome skunks of major proportions, might be stalking the banks in search of freshwater crustaceans.

I am never sure of the nature of a river when it breaks away from the direction I am traveling. What secrets are out there, if any? The wonder and magic of exploring creeks when I was a child has been a life-long fascination.

That evening a hatch of mayflies that were too big to be *baetis* and definitely were not green drakes (that is as close as I am going to get to trying to match the hatch) was rising from the river. They were about size 14 and grayish-brown, a pattern that precisely matched several species of patterns I had in fly boxes scattered throughout my vest. Rapidly approaching fly fishing sophistication and panache, I tied on a twelve-foot, 6X leader and cast the thing across to and well above a feeding trout. The leader and fluffy fly collapsed gracefully in a pile of coils that rode jauntily on the surface. The flyline was floating drag free and the leader was extended for perhaps seven of its twelve feet. It was a perfect cast, and I decided to ride the sucker out to its conclusion.

An imperceptible ripple in the current spun the fly around several times so that there was now almost two feet of straight monofilament between the fly and the heap. The hackles graced the scene with a certain flair, passing directly through the brown's feeding lane. Suddenly the fly was no longer there. Gone just like my tent. The merest dimple of a rise spread out and down the river. The hook set itself, and the brown leaped twice, taking enough line with it that I was now playing the fish from the reel. I had not moved a muscle. This was really my kind of fishing—full-bore vegematic synchronicity loose on the Musselshell.

Coming alive, I palmed the reel carefully during each of a series of short runs climaxed with a serious head shaking that drummed its angry message up through the line. Then two more leaps and two more quick bursts that took the trout under some exposed tree roots. I thought the game was lost, but the brown turned and raced right back at me, carving a wake in the liquid light as the firm connection with the fish went slack. Still more coils, this time flyline, piled up at my feet as I madly stripped the stuff through the guides.

I reestablished contact with the fish, which was now right in front of me, listing slightly and checking out the situation with one dark eye. Leaning over, I gripped the brown behind the head first with one hand and then with both. Maybe twenty inches, but size was unimportant. Wide, thick, very alive with colors that glowed in the fading light. Just that great brown trout and me, standing alone in this wonderfully strange river.

Big Spring Creek

*U*nless you are a big game or upland bird hunter, you probably have not been to the Lewistown, Montana, area. For the fly fisher, other portions of the Big Sky State hold more, bigger, and better-known trout waters than are found here. That's fine and understandable, but something of a shame because there is a stream that offers some pretty fair angling in this neck of the high plains: Big Spring Creek.

Many of those who devote sizeable portions of their lives to chasing trout know about the stream. Most of the rest of us bumble along in benign ignorance. Flowing for twenty miles or so to its confluence with the milky Judith River and then on into Missouri River turbidity somewhere north of the small town of Winifred, Big Spring Creek has healthy populations of rainbows and browns along with a few cutthroats, brooks, and much-maligned whitefish tossed in for the sake of variety.

The stream, averaging twenty-five to thirty-five feet wide and two feet deep with some big holes, tumbles down from some gentle hills outside of Lewistown and then wanders casually through open pasture and rangeland spread out below the Big Snowy, Judith, and Little Belt mountain ranges.

Because these fish receive quite a bit of pressure (by nobody-comes-here-much Montana standards) and because the water is so clear, it is impossible to hide a tactical mistake. The fishing is deceptive in its studied and difficult intensity. That's fine, too. The duration of the attraction of anything pleasurable in this life seems to be in inverse proportion to its availability and accessibility (the Cubs winning a World Series comes to mind).

Lewistown anglers, when they're not chasing game in the mountains or fishing monstrous ranch-pond trout on the breezy prairie, spend a good deal of time on this water, with bountiful results. There are a bunch of rainbows in the one- to two-pound range and a sizeable gang of browns finning about in the three-pound vicinity. An average day on the water will certainly yield at least one decent fish, if diligence is applied to the activity.

Big Spring Creek, just below town, flows through pastureland with some trees lining the banks here and there. This stretch is easy to wade and casting room is abundant. The first time I fished the water it was near sunset, and the surrounding mountains were radiating that special orange softness common to a sun dropping beneath a western horizon. Trout were rising everywhere to small caddis, but as I quickly learned, one chance was all an angler received for making a proper presentation.

Any offering wildly out of line with accepted streamside behavior put the fish down. Yet if the fly reached the water's surface with some degree of grace and dignity and then managed to drift through a trout's field of vision, the take was quick and sure and the fight spirited.

An hour and a half spent working runs, glides, and current seams adjacent to riffles produced a dozen rainbows and a brace of browns in the twelve- to fourteen-inch range, with one fish pushing a foot and a half. These were beautiful, robust trout. The rainbows were fat and silvery, with a lovely splash of iridescent pink along their flanks. The browns were more elongated, but muscular and shaded with browns and golds and the blackest of spotting.

This experience, coupled with the excellent hunting for sharptail and sage grouse, Hungarian partridge, and pheasant I'd experienced east of town over by Sweetgrass, made Lewistown look like my conception of perfection. Subsequent excursions have only added to these fond impressions.

Big Spring Creek is formed at a spot about eight miles east of town where fifty-two-degree water gushes from the ground at over 50,000 gallons per minute. The water here is saturated with nitrogen, which contributes to sparse fish numbers in the first few yards of the stream.

Located at this site is the Big Springs Fish Hatchery, where half of the state's rainbows come into existence. Five strains, including Arlee and Eagle Lake, are raised at the facility, and you might run into any of them in the water immediately below the hatchery.

The creek can be divided into two sections. A classic and very difficult to fish spring creek stretch is above town (the hatchery section, I suppose), and a less clear, somewhat easier to fish run, with more and bigger trout, is below town. Complicating the upper stretch are banks that are choked with dense brush, while the lower water is more wide open in nature, making for easier casting.

According to Steve Leathe of the Montana Department of Fish, Wildlife and Parks, the upper water has between 300 and 700 catchable rainbows and about 100 browns per mile. But the biggest fish in the creek, probably escapees from the hatchery, are lying in some deep holes up here, virtually impossible to catch. The number of trout per mile in the lower stretch is remarkable. Consider these numbers from a 1986 survey for rainbows: five to ten inches—1,500; ten to fifteen inches—1,500; greater than fifteen inches—90. According to Leathe, there are also 300 to 500 brown trout exceeding ten inches for each stream mile.

"The fish are there, but they are extremely tough to catch and you don't see that many over sixteen inches," said Leathe. "There's one stretch that has so many fish, you'd figure you'd snag one using a nymph, but I got skunked. You've really got to know what you are doing to take fish here."

Learning to fish this water on your own is frustrating. Some of my attempts in the past had yielded, at best, pathetic results despite superb casts to the easy-to-spot feeding fish in the upper section. Then fate took a hand and I bumped into a local legend (or so I'm told by unreliable

Big Spring Creek.

sources in town), the now late Jack Pittman, who made some money tying flies and fished Big Spring Creek "a couple of hundred days a year." Pittman had done this for three and a half decades, so a very conservative and rough estimate of his time on the water weighs in at around 15,000 hours. Pittman's strategy is simple: "Nymphs in the fast water and dries on the flats." Good advice, but I discovered that being able to cast a 7'9", two-weight rod like a demon helps considerably.

This fertile flow is home to abundant insect life, but matching the hatch is a straightforward proposition. Caddis imitations from March through November, black stone flies from late March into early April, tricos from mid-August through September, and grasshoppers beginning in August and running until the hard frosts set in. Throw in a beggar's banquet of terrestrials such as ants and beetles and you've covered a lot of the possibilities.

What adds some serious spice to this fishing is the pace of the current—four to six feet per second—coupled with a host of surface and subsurface variations. This is benthic madness for the purveyor of nymphs.

Less than a perfect presentation equals zero trout. Many of the best fish hold tight to the brush-covered, undercut banks (would good trout anywhere have it any other way?), where the water zips by like a carefree teenager on the prowl at the local mall. Mid-air mends and judicious use of body English are required to attain even a brief drag-free float. And these fish are wary.

One afternoon, Pittman said that I "spooked half the damn trout in the creek," and I only saw half of those. "You've got to be careful," said Pittman. "Don't get too close to the fish. They can see you from a long way away in this water."

Stalking and making casts from a crouched position are a big part of the game at Big Spring Creek, but casts over forty feet are uncommon due to the brushy banks and the circuitous personality of the creek.

The creek is open all year. Starting in September you can count on hatches of mayflies and caddis beginning around high noon and lasting until 4:00 P.M. Obviously, the biggest fish prefer to practice their cannibalistic ways under the protective cover of darkness, but at this time of the year and during these hours of the day, some surprisingly big trout are on the move. We watched one feeding in a shaded curl of bank across from us for several minutes before Pittman whipped a cast just above the lie with a two-weight outfit whose cork grip showed the wear that comes from good use. The rainbow blasted the Blue-Winged Olive, lifting off well above the turquoise water and then struggling upstream before coming back down current to us. A good fish, maybe seventeen inches, but extremely husky and almost two pounds. Pittman referred to the trout's rotund girth as "pathetic," but you have to fish with the guy to appreciate his humor.

On one run of about fifty yards, Pittman worked a dry first, taking four trout in the twelve- to fourteen-inch range. Next, I plodded through with a weighted nymph on a short line and took four more in the same size range.

All of the creek's forks and tributaries have decent angling possibilities, but a large portion of the water around here is on private land. Fortunately, there is plenty of access from County Road 238, which parallels much of the upper stretch, including the area at Brewery Flats just outside of town near the less than scenic Burlington Northern property. Ugly or not, this is prime brown trout turf. There are also places to get to the river below town where County Road 426 crosses the stream here and there.

If one rod was all you could bring to fish this water, it would have to be the 7'9", two-weight item with the ever-popular weight-forward line. This outfit is ideal for the necessary delicate casts and offers dandy sport considering the average size of the trout. I've been playing around with a 7'11", four-weight on the creek, and the setup is a bit more forgiving than the lighter rig but not too much rod or line weight for the stream.

We used 4X and 5X tippets on nine-foot leaders, but 6X on twelve-footers would be better. (It didn't seem to matter to Pittman. He caught every fish he cast to and selected the trout he planned to work on with studied indifference.)

In addition to Blue-Winged Olives, Elk Hair Caddis, Red Quills, Lt. Cahills, PMDs, and Adamses will work. Hare's Ear Nymphs and similar dressings produce, as do black ant patterns. I have a fondness for Goddard Caddis, which in #16–18 drifted through the fastest stretches and caught rainbows.

To take a legitimate shot at big browns (over four pounds on rare occasions), try the water from mid-October on into the nastiness of November using big Woolly Buggers in the time-honored "chuck-and-duck" methods. Pittman says he takes his largest trout using Buggers on lousy, mean-spirited afternoons. He also mentioned that he has taken some big fish during January and February bluebird days on Midges. Days in the fifties are not unheard of here in the winter when a warm-headed Chinook rips down along the mountains from somewhere up in the Canadian provinces.

Basically, the water is fishable year-round, except for a very brief period of unsettledness during spring runoff. The constant temperature of the spring-fed water ensures a productive environment for aquatic life twelve months a year.

Oh, yes. About those "monstrous" ranch-pond trout. Access to private waters is the stuff of rare good fortune, but a couple of small lakes about ten miles north of town on U.S. 191 will give you a little taste of what this species of angling can be like. Upper and Lower Carter's Ponds are both shallow, less than fifteen acres, and absolutely jam-packed with freshwater shrimp. Walk into the water. Walk back out and look at your waders. They'll be covered with the dull-green creatures, and the trout love them.

Both ponds are located out in the open rangeland and, as a result, are susceptible to high winds, but they do contain some nice rainbows in the three- to four-pound class that are catchable when the winds don't blow. Scud patterns and bold attention-getting streamers cast from shore or from float tubes and then stripped back will sometimes entice the gorged trout.

I got lucky (a true rarity) one day with Jack and his buddy, Jack Spicir. They told me I had a "pair of Jacks to draw to" and then broke into laughter as we wailed down a state highway well over what was then the posted speed limit waving at state troopers going the other way. (In many parts of Montana, local residents consider the speed limit more of a suggestion than a mandate.) I was informed that we were in hot pursuit of "a bunch of big god-damned rainbows."

A couple of dusty gravel-road turnoffs later found us parked above a ranch pond of maybe a couple of acres or so. The only sounds were those of the Wagoneer's motor cooling and the busy harvesting sounds of strong machinery in nearby fields. High plains Montana drifted off in all directions, golden and ablaze in the autumn, late-day light.

By the time I had tied a large Girdle Bug to a 2X tippet as I was in-structed to do by the two Jacks, Spicir was already fighting a rainbow just below me. Thrashing the surface and shaking its head, the trout was well over twenty inches and heavy. Ten minutes and a few casts later I had already caught three trout in the five-pound range, but the Jacks decided we should head off to another out-of-the-way pond and try for some "big" fish.

We lurched and bounced our way several miles over dirt field-roads and started casting as darkness set in. But we got skunked and gave it up in the chilling night air.

"Hell, I haven't fished here this year," groused Pittman. "Some-body probably caught all the damn fish. Let's go home."

"You're crazy. Nobody could catch every damn fish here," snapped Spicir. "And just wait a minute and let's have a beer." Which we did and then drove home dodging countless deer browsing next to the highway. The gentle mountains surrounding town glowed in the starlight.

And that's about the shape of things in Lewistown. The rest is up to individual curiosity, determination, and the fly fishing gods . . . and maybe a couple of jokers named Jack.

Missouri River

*T*he Missouri is a good river for a fly fisher, one of the best trout streams in North America. The river surges into being at Three Forks right next to the fast-paced madness of Interstate 90. Three very fine trout waters—the Jefferson, Madison, and Gallatin rivers—combine to make this a world-class environment for trout.

From this point for over 150 miles downstream, mostly north to just south of Great Falls, is some of the finest fishing for rainbow and brown trout in the world. A good day during the summer can mean plenty of fish over a pound and a few over three.

In the fall, however, you are not after numbers. You are looking for the one trout that all others you have caught or will ever catch will be compared with. It will be ten pounds or more. Maybe you will never catch it, or maybe you will after a couple of cold, wet, frustrating seasons. Or perhaps it will appear on the first cast of a clear October morning.

The Missouri takes its time drifting through wide-open valleys defined by geologic structures with names like Giant Hill, Lava Mountain, Horseshoe Hills, and Hogback Mountain. Grouse, elk, and mountain lions roam the high forests and parklike meadows. Cattle, pheasant, and deer thrive in the cultivated fields of alfalfa and timothy in the fertile flatland. Here and there huge amalgams of sticks, straw, and even roadside litter are spotted perched atop telephone poles that have lost their perpendicular touch with the earth—osprey nests.

A few dams slow the river even more and form large bodies of water: Canyon Ferry Lake, Hauser Lake, and Holter Lake. Big trout hold in places such as these until the spawning imperative drives them out of deepwater sanctuary on a biologically forced march up-river to ancient breeding grounds.

A few miles above the small town of Toston and along the fifty-five winding miles between Helena and Hardy, the Missouri forces itself through wild twistings and striations of limestone rock formations that were part of a vast inland sea 100 million years ago. This is canyon country now.

Interstate 15 and many lesser roads bend and swerve to the will of these harsh walls of ochre, pink, red, and oxidized green. Clumps of pine grow to the edge of elaborate rock outcroppings, clinging pre-cariously to existence, with gnarled roots dangling in free space. Openings to abandoned mine shafts pockmark the cliffs.

Small creeks called Prickly Pear, Wolf, and Sixteen Mile make their way down to the river. There are trout here, too, and they are often large. There are also rattlesnakes and bighorn sheep, and eagles that sometimes glide by so closely you can hear the air breaking over their wings.

Every fly fisher should make at least one trip to this stretch of the Missouri, where there is an abundance of angling opportunity and va-riety in the runs and pools.

Still more fishing is waiting far off in the distance. Several hundred lonely miles to the east, below mammoth Fort Peck Dam, steelhead-like rainbows thrive in a fresh, clear tailwater fishery, mostly unknown and only rarely fished over with a fly. Very real trout magic lies out there on the arid, high plains. But first, there is much to be learned of the Missouri by fishing between Three Forks and Great Falls.

"It's like fishing for sharks. You know there are big fish here," said guide Paul Roos. "Searching for them gets in your blood."

Roos quietly worked the oars as our raft drifted casually down this stretch of the Missouri. Cliffs, bluffs, and hills, their vegetation turned raw sienna by crisp late-October nights, rose high above us. A few puffy clouds plied their trade in a limitless sky. It was just nine in the morning, but the air was already pleasantly warm. It was a beautiful day to be on the river, but not the nasty, snow-flecked weather needed to start the big browns moving up from Canyon Ferry on their annual spawning runs, a twenty-mile jaunt that produces some of the finest trophy trout fishing in the world.

My companion in the front of the raft hammered the brushy banks and deep eddies with what looked like a "large, green, hairy bug." In reality it was a Woolly Bugger, one of the more productive patterns on the Missouri. "Some oldtimers use nothing else here," said Roos.

Line whistled by from another quick cast to a promising pocket under a clump of bushes. On the second strip of line, a brown nailed the fly. A short but strong fight brought a fat, fifteen-inch trout to net. Not great size-wise, but a nice fish all the same. What we were chasing were large—make that *very* large—brown trout. Fish that often exceed ten pounds and will occasionally top fifteen pounds. "Browns to ten pounds," was the phrase often heard from another member of the trip.

From mid-October through November these fish move upriver from several large reservoirs to their spawning grounds, with large redds marking their locations. Earlier in the year there is plenty of fishing for resident trout that will often exceed several pounds. I've taken decent fish on dries and nymphs all through the river in July and August, but fall is special. It's big-time trout-hunting season.

Neither the brown trout nor the rainbow trout population is natural here. The browns are self-sustaining, but the rainbow numbers are augmented by a vigorous stocking program conducted by the state.

The Montana Department of Fish, Wildlife and Parks plants thousands of rainbows in the impoundments along the river and in a few sections of the Missouri itself. With the discovery of whirling disease in the Madison River, and now many other waters both east and west of the Continental Divide, the future of Montana's rainbow fishery is in serious jeopardy. The disease affects the skeletal structure of young fish, causing them to swim erratically or in circles, hence the name

Working the Missouri River near Cascade on a July afternoon.

of the affliction. This makes the trout easy prey for predators, and many of the sick fish are unable to feed and die of starvation. There is no cure for whirling disease short of drying up a river and fumigating the streambed. Resistant strains of rainbows will more than likely need to be planted in the future to maintain the resource, but the outlook is grim at best. As many as 90 percent of the rainbows have vanished from some stretches of the Madison River and a similar scenario is not unlikely for other rivers. Happy trails.

On sunny days, the fish will hug the brush-covered, undercut banks, afraid to expose themselves to predators in the bright light. But when the weather becomes overcast, wet, and nasty, the big browns throw caution to the winds and move out onto their redds, thus providing top-notch action for large fish.

Earlier in the fall we had fished a section of the river south of Great Falls around Cascade. Despite the clouds, wind, and low water, we managed to catch a number of hefty rainbows and browns on small *baetis* spinner imitations. The fishing suddenly turned on and for two hours we could not miss. Then the trout stopped feeding. They just quit, and nothing we did could alter that fact of river life.

The section of the river we were fishing that October day was from the put-in just below Toston Dam down to the takeout at Toston, about forty-five minutes from the state capital of Helena.

In one section of the Missouri, recent electrofishing surveys indicated 2,500 catchable trout per mile and over 100 fish exceeding eighteen inches. This is a river where the amount of trout per mile is measured in tons, not pounds. Because of the barrier presented by Toston Dam and the large numbers of fish in Canyon Ferry, the stretch of river from Townsend to the impoundment most likely contains the highest concentration of large fish. But the fishing from below Holter Dam for ninety miles to Great Falls will hold its own with the upper stretch. The main difference is that the number of rainbows far exceeds the number of browns.

Even though the weather was magnificent, the fishing was tough, as it usually is when you chase big fish. You're here because there is a very real chance to turn twelve pounds of determined brown trout muscle fighting for its life and perhaps for an even stronger imperative, procreation, at the end of a 1X tippet.

Sounds large, doesn't it? Well, when a monster brown boils the water near the bank as it inhales your streamer and then heads fast, fast, fast downriver, any tippet, no matter how strong, will seem woefully inadequate. This is not "rod bent double as it horses a two-pound fish to the raft to be netted prior to release." No, this is lunatic behavior that frequently goes unrewarded. What's going on here is hanging on for dear life while the guide frantically (yet skillfully, of course) beaches the craft as you clamber over the side and hit the ground running, stumbling, and tripping after a trout gone berserk with all the finesse of a runaway freight train. Admittedly, this doesn't happen often. In fact, the experience failed to materialize for me that particular autumn day. But when it does happen, maybe once a year, maybe once every decade, the thousands of casts, the bone-chilling damp weather, and yes, the boredom, all vanish somewhere back upriver.

This is classic big water—maybe 3,000 to 4,000 cfs even at this time of the year. The Missouri begins life with the pure waters that originate as snowmelt high in the rugged mountains of the Yellowstone National Park region. The waters of the Missouri are full of nutrients and aquatic life—tricos, caddis, stone flies, mayflies, crane flies, small forage fish. Everything the trout need to grow fat and happy, which they do with a vengeance.

From September through early October, *baetis* will emerge from late morning until around four in the afternoon. Nymphs prefer the faster water but have adapted to almost any flow the Missouri offers. The dun is probably the most important stage for the angler, but the nymph just prior to the time of emergence, caught in the surface film, can also take trout. The size range varies from #16–24, with the smaller patterns being more prevalent in the fall.

Tricos hatch in the late spring and early summer and again in late summer and early fall (August through September). This hatch usually is too soon to match the fall run of the larger fish, but it provides plenty of action for the smaller one- to three-pounders during the morning hours. These tricos tend to run a little larger in the Missouri, according to Rick Pasquale of Fly Fisher's Retreat in Great Falls. By larger, he means maybe #18–22 instead of #20–26. Recognizing trico spinners is relatively easy. They are small, of course. They have three tails, with the male's about three times the length of its body and the female's the same length as her body. The wings are clear and there are no hind wings, unlike most mayflies.

On a river where 1X tippets are common, fishing with the diminutive sizes required to properly present a #22 dry is a challenge and a trade-off. Large tippets needed to hold large fish won't allow the fly to turn over and will spook the trout. But the tiny tippets needed for accurate presentation will more often than not break off when connected to a big brown or rainbow. It's the classic angling paradox, and it surfaces repeatedly on the Missouri River.

The most comfortable rod-line combination for me is an 8'6" or 9'0" rod with either a six- or seven-weight forward line. Some very good fishermen go up to eight-weight, probably a plus on blustery days that make casting a nightmare. But this has always seemed too cumbersome and tiring for me. It's all a matter of personal preference.

Local experts and fish and game officials think an angler will some-day land a fish in the twenty-pound range, more than likely directly below one of the dams. I think they are right. When you are floating along with the deceptively powerful current, you can feel, or sense, the giant fish holding in the calmer bottom flows beneath the surface. Casting to likely-looking spots is actually scary at times, the fish move so quickly and are so strong.

On the October trip, I cast a large Woolly Bugger to a foam-covered eddy. Before I could even start stripping in the line, a monstrous fish boiled, its dorsal fin rising several inches above the water. My shocked strike missed the fish, and my nerves were rattled.

"Move pretty quickly, don't they?" laughed Roos.

The flies are big, size #4 and larger, and they often have a small split shot or two cinched in at the head of the pattern. Casting these with any accuracy requires a good deal of practice and patience.

Much of my fishing is done on the small streams and mountain lakes in the northwest corner of the state, where #18 and smaller are common. Here I was using a 9'0" rod with seven-weight line; back home I usually play with a 7'6", four-weight outfit. A big adjustment on my part was necessary, and, fortunately, Roos guided me through the transition with a smile, saying he felt that his life was in danger that day only "once or twice."

Add to the equation sleet and wind, as we experienced the next day, and casting becomes sporting at best. One day in a gale, the two of us in the boat made use of a sidearm sling-type cast that more closely resembled a marine lobbing a hand grenade into an enemy pillbox. It was an ugly technique to be sure, but it was the only way to cheat the wind and put the fly flush to the bank where the browns were located. There were times when we turned fish of three pounds or better in only a few inches of water. You wondered why you couldn't spot their fins waving back and forth above the surface. After the cast is made, a quick stripping of the line in about two-foot lengths is made until the cast is fished out. The browns will often follow the fly right up to the raft before taking—a heart-stopping experience.

The most common mistake an angler makes on the Missouri is not getting the fly to the bottom where the fish are. Casts quartering up-stream help, as do high-density sinking-tip lines or the addition of lead above a fly when using a floating line. Another key is under-standing the level of flow, which is controlled by the amount of water released at the various dams by the powers that be. As a result, fish-ing can be great one day and off the next when the river level rises quickly and unnaturally.

Brown trout are no more predictable than any other salmonid species, so the speed and the depth of the retrieve needs constant modification until the right combination is found. The same is true of fly selection. Patterns such as the Woolly Bugger take very big fish, and Roos pointed out that color is often critical. He suggested an olive body as the prime choice, followed by black and even all white. Other choices include a yellow Maribou Muddler or a black-on-white item, and patterns that include the Matuka Spruce, sculpin imitations, Gir-dle Bugs, and Zonkers work well. For *baetis* I prefer David Hughes's pattern, the Little Olive Parachute, and an olive nymph in a compa-rable size. And for the tricos, a poly-wing spinner.

The basic mechanics of trophy brown fishing are relatively easy to master, but to excel an angler must work long and hard, learning the little nuances that turn a zero fish day into something memorable.

One of the keys to this kind of fishing is actually believing both that fish are present when none are seen rising and that they are catch-able. At first glance the Missouri can be intimidating. It's hundreds of feet wide and fairly deep, but this vastness is rapidly reduced to pock-ets along the banks, deep runs, riffles, and holes around boulders.

A couple of miles below where my friend caught his brown, we pulled over to a gravel bar to fish the numerous good-looking holes. Roos rigged up a rod and went downstream. I paused in my fishing to watch him work a deep run. Long, straight casts rocketed out over the water before settling softly on the surface. What happened next is etched in my mind. Roos bent over from the waist in a crouch, quickly and intently stripping the line. He looked as though he had shifted his awareness to the fly, not just thinking where it was and what it was doing along the bottom, but actually swimming along with it down there.

On the third cast he swiftly pulled the rod back, and a large brown rose up and thrashed along the surface. This was something of a revelation to me; I always thought browns fought below the water. On this trip a majority of the fish fought like rainbows. After several strong, acrobatic runs, Roos brought the fish to shore. It was over two feet and maybe six pounds. A very good fish by any standards.

Later, as the float neared an end, I stopped fishing and just sat back enjoying the river and the changing light on the slopes around us. This is what hunting big fish is all about. Open country rolling off for miles to distant mountains and a big, graceful river to fish.

Each year when the larch starts to bud on my side of the mountains, I load up the truck and head east to challenge the other part of the Missouri, the stretch that has rainbow trout and is so far away from "trout country" that it is virtually unknown and unfished by those with fly rods.

I never thought I'd be talking fly fishing with a bunch of paleontologists while standing on the roof of some guy's house that was covered with several tons of moss agate. But that is precisely what I was doing on this very hot late-spring night in eastern Montana just outside of Glendive. The sound of the Yellowstone River rushing bankfull and muddy with snowmelt filled in the occasional conversational gaps. Smoke from my cigar rose straight up into the sky.

When the water level of the river drops, countless gem-quality agates are left exposed on gravel bars beneath a vicious sun. Rejects ("leverites" in the local comedic idiom, as in "Leave it right where you found it") are abundant. The rather bizarre collection scattered about my feet was ample proof of a geologic fecundity.

The paleontologists had not seen a lot of people lately. They'd been living in tepees and bathing in a watering tank, so they were having a good time drinking and talking about fly fishing.

I was beginning to suspect that maybe they'd spent perhaps a bit too much time out on the plains brushing fine sediment from dinosaur bones with camel hair paint brushes. Right in the middle of a sentence at least one of them would suddenly cease talking and stare off into space. This can be disconcerting, and when five of them do it at once, looking at God-knows-what in the West, I find myself edging toward the saner elements of the cocktail party swirling below me on the lawn.

During their brief interludes of lucidity they tipped me to some fabulous fishing for big, wild rainbow trout swimming away ninety miles north of this party in a tailwater below Fort Peck Dam. When I confronted my host with this information he in turn confronted me with some out-of-focus color prints showing him hoisting a brace of hefty rainbow trout that had passed the five-pound range a few seasons back.

My immediate questions of where, when, and how were ignored as he built me another punch-bowl-sized martini, laughing quietly all the while. I took the drink with both hands, and he joined a group of people who were smoking cigarettes and discussing cattle futures. The remainder of the evening was fun but not exceptionally productive.

When I returned home several days later I called a friend, Pat Clancey, who worked for the Montana Department of Fish, Wildlife and Parks at Fort Peck. He confirmed my wife's worst fears. "Hell, yes, there's rainbow here in the tailwater and they run between 4 and 7 1/2 pounds, and I've never seen anyone fish for them with a fly rod." Further investigation revealed that a few local meat fishermen using doorknobs for sinkers and dead skunks for bait occasionally took a few of these trout, but that was about the extent of the sport fishing for rainbows over there. Presently this is an extremely fragile population that cannot stand much pressure, but Clancey and his professional peers hold out some hope that the rainbow numbers are growing slowly and will someday represent at least the illusion of permanence.

An added bonus is that this fishing is just 500 miles away, a straight shot on U.S. 2 from my home in northwestern Montana across the wide-open turf along the highline into Glasgow (population 4,455 and civilization), and then a breezy drive along state highway 24 to Fort Peck, Pat Clancey, and those big rainbows. At eighty miles an hour I can make the drive in under seven hours.

Fort Peck Dam is earthen in nature and so big that when the thing was being built in the thirties a huge chunk of it became saturated with water and calmly slid a quarter of a mile out into the reservoir filling behind it, taking men and machines with it. The dam is 6 miles long with a highway running across the top. When you pull over you can look back west across much of the 189-mile length of Fort Peck Lake. Most of the time when you do this the wind will try to blow you down the hill and into the Missouri pouring out onto the plains hundreds of feet below. Moving, rushing air is a constant, palpable existence in eastern Montana. The wind has literally driven men insane, causing them to commit violent acts against their neighbors.

The river is big here, too big to successfully fish the main channel. You have to cut the water down to a manageable size, and this is done by working a side channel, which is best done in the spring. Rainbows are on the move at this time, and there is sufficient flow to float you over some gravel bars. The water is anywhere from 100 to 200 yards wide. The trout hold out in deep (eight feet or more) runs and chutes. This is where you will fish your streamer. A one-mile section of prime spawning habitat is off limits to the attentions of anglers. Big signs make sure you are aware of this fact.

I've fished here three times and have two fish to show for my efforts, but they were both over four pounds, and when hooked they went body-smacking and tailwalking across the water like enraged Brahma bulls at a rodeo.

"Three thousand miles of driving for two fish," my friends and wife exclaim. "Holt, you really are nuts."

Why deny truth? The Fort Peck tailwater is what Montana trout hunting is all about for me. Middle-of-nowhere fishing for unreal fish with nothing but nothing flowing into 360 degrees of empty, windy, dusty distance. There is freedom and wonder way out there.

Up above there are guys trolling on the lake for walleyes with weighted license plates. If you like this kind of activity, I'm told the fishing is quite good. They even have a Governor's Cup Walleye Tournament. I don't know anything about that stuff. The rainbows are my game, one that rarely needs to be shared with the occasional bait fisherman, who, I've discovered, will often know the holding areas inside and out.

Clancey says that the only aquatic insect life of any note is chironomid and dipteran in nature, which more or less eliminates matching the hatch. The water is deep and the fish concentrate on forage species, according to the biologist's research.

The fish I took hammered a #2 Zonker and a similar-sized sculpin imitation fished with a couple of lead twist-ons and worked with a fast-sinking line and a short (four feet), stout (1X) leader.

Even in the best of conditions this is a tough, often unpleasant, business. When you factor in gusting winds that come at you in puffs strong enough to force you to shift your feet to maintain balance, you're talking austere angling conditions, especially from a boat. You can handle some of the water from shore, but a stable flat-bottom craft will give you a decent casting platform away from bankside obstructions, and you can fish the water thoroughly.

Clancey knows where the fish are, and everything I know about chasing the rainbows here (and it is not a lot, yet) comes from him or from experience.

Maybe someday I'll see these unique fish rise to flies on the surface, and that would be fine fishing, but until such time, I'll content myself with devoting one long, hard day each year to drifting streamers down along the river's bottom.

The rainbows will hit if the pattern passes in front of them. When they do it is a hell of a sight to watch Montana's version of a steelhead race across the river with nothing but the hills and bluffs of the high plains fading away into the deserted horizon.

South Fork of the Flathead River

*T*oo damn easy, I thought. The Sofa Pillow never had a chance. Five, six feet of drift at the most before a fat westslope cutthroat, or two or three, broke through the surface and drilled the bushy pattern. The trout would then sound using the strong current as leverage, but the fight was useless. A dead issue. Several runs of shortening duration and the fish came to me. Fifteen inches. Up to twenty inches. On each cast.

A long, deep run with swirling eddies and braided seams of current created by submerged rocks created enough holding water for a hundred cutthroat. I'd never seen such eager or beautiful trout take flies with such abandon. Already a dozen or so had been caught and all but three released. Dinnertime considerations led to the swift death of the trio.

Amy and I hiked in here, a three-day jaunt, with packs that seemed to weigh two hundred pounds, but were closer to seventy, holding provisions for a few weeks hiking the backcountry of the Bob Marshall Wilderness in northwest Montana. Stories of the South Fork of the Flathead River and its outrageous cutthroat fishing were common. This was back in the early seventies before hordes of guided rafters, dudes on horseback, and neophyte backpackers had turned the area into a zoo. Along for the ride was my Irish Wolfhound, Bonzo, a happy soul with gaze-hound tendencies. A fine companion.

141

We set up a basic camp that warm July afternoon. Tent, cooking area—the usual stuff. I immediately clambered down a bouldery bank to the river and began catching trout on the first cast. This was amazing. Special. You always hear about how some place has fishing so good that it becomes boring after a couple of hours. Untrue. I fished for over eight hours, taking well over one hundred fish as I worked my way up and down the river. Any cast, whether it was filled with drag or hampered by coiled line, raised trout. Nice strong ones full of silvers, black-blues, golds, crimsons, black spots, and riotous orange cuts along their jaws. I'd never experienced fly fishing like this and only have a few times in the years since. Any fly I tied on worked—Adams, Royal Wulffs, hoppers, a red and black deerhair bass bug, streamers of gaudy construction. It didn't matter. The fish were wild, undisciplined, and easy to fool. And every now and then a mountain whitefish of two pounds or more would enter the fray and suck in my fly. I kept two of these. Food for the dog.

I was only twenty-one back then. Hair down to the middle of my back (it's mostly gone now), in good shape, and totally unaware of the hardships and pain of day-to-day living that awaited me. Amy was the same age, with long golden hair, beautiful deep blue eyes, and a personality that turned me helpless. No responsibilities. No worries. Great country. An even greater woman. Why did I have to grow up? I knew someday I would have to at least pretend to be a responsible adult (later I realized that I really didn't), but for now I was full-tilt hedonistic on every level I was aware of and some that I wasn't hip to but that were present just the same.

The South Fork heads high in the mountains of the Scapegoat Wilderness, about twenty miles upstream of where I was playing, and flows for over fifty miles to its confluence with the main stem of the Flathead. Crystal clear (sapphire tinged with emerald) water all the way. Clear liquid that pours over a rocky streambed filled with soft reds, ochre, greens, blues, grays, and browns. The sound of the moving water was the best of natural music. The river is deceptive in its depth and power. People unfamiliar with mountain rivers are washed away on an unexpected ride to the next world each year. Where the water looks three feet deep, it is often six or more. Where it appears six feet, it will kill you. Cold, fast-moving, uncaring; an honest river running through ponderosa and lodgepole pine. Mountains everywhere. A thousand-foot rocky escarpment, the Chinese Wall, holds forth on the eastern horizon. Grizzlies, black bears, elk as big as pack horses, martens, hoary marmots, eagles, three-toed woodpeckers, big cats, bull trout to twenty pounds, and even hummingbirds. Not a bad place to disappear.

Trails reach the interior of South Fork country from the Swan Valley in the west, along the Rocky Mountain Front in the east, through the Scapegoat in the south, and via Hungry Horse Reservoir-Slowly-Turning-Mud-Pit in the north. The dam, completed in the fifties, wiped out more than thirty miles of this untamed river, and each year when the U.S. Army Corps of Engineers draws the thing down in the summer for power generation, Hungry Horse looks like an anorexic pond bent on a lingering suicide. An ugly mess that our taxes paid for and we have no control over.

With all the fishing pressure that peaked in the eighties, the numbers and size of the native cutthroat dropped dramatically, but slot limits and stronger catch-and-release regulations have improved the fishing. Not as good as when I was a crazed hipster, but still pretty damn fair. A nine-foot five-weight, some 4X tippet, a haphazard assortment of dries, streamers, and nymphs, and if you don't catch a fish, take up lawn darts.

Bonzo was up on the bank watching me kill the whitefish. He had correctly guessed that these were his dinner. We built a fire and cooked the trout along with some wild rice and pasta. We ate like starving wolves and watched the moon rise over the Chinese Wall, then went into the tent. About an hour later the weirdest, almost subliminal of sounds came from near the fire.

The South Fork of the Flathead River.

"What the hell's that?" Amy asked in some alarm.

"Beats me, but I'll check." The strange, cushioned sound of almost desperate screeching was starting to get on my nerves. As I crawled out into the cool air, a soft breeze dried the sweat on my body. In the moonlight I saw several large porcupines crawling around our gear. They were almost alien in appearance and movement. We should have hung the stuff from a tree limb, but I forgot. I picked up a large rock and heaved it at one of the animals that was perched on my already battered Kelty pack. I missed the porcupine, but a sharp tinkling sound of breaking glass and crunched metal indicated I'd managed to nail my camera. Damn! The porkies ambled off and I went back in to Amy. The next morning I examined the remains of my mangled Bessler TopCon camera. I'd reduced it to junk. No more photos this trip.

Things got better. Around noon, a game warden rode up; he was wearing state trooper sunglasses, a real neat uniform, and a .357 magnum. Way back in the middle of nowhere and some fool was copping a Dirty Harry attitude. He examined both of our licenses and eyed Amy far more than I cared for.

"You checked us out. Anything else?" I asked, the implications in the question obvious, and I was getting mad as hell. "Nothing like getting away from it all back here."

"You've got a smart mouth, kid," the trooper sneered.

"And you're a public servant with shit for brains," I replied. Crazy and foolish back then.

"Maybe you'd like to carry the conversation to the next level."

I was ready and way over my red line. "You watch too many movies, but, yah, why the hell not, Ace."

Fortunately for me, Amy jumped into the fray with three warm beers, a winning smile, and some vibes that cooled out what promised to be an unpleasant situation. In a matter of seconds, she had the trooper calmed down and eating out of her hand. She was a master at this sort of thing, but the way she spun people around never ceased to astound me. After a while he mounted his horse and rode off into the pines.

"John, that was a dumbass move, even by your standards."

"I know, Amy. Sorry and thanks," but she stayed mad for a couple more hours, so the hound and I did a lot of walking and fishing on our own. Some of us have the knack of screwing up with frightening consistency.

A few days later, tranquillity and harmony restored, we headed out of the wilderness, up the Holbrook Creek Trail. Fifteen miles to the divide and then on down to Upper Holland Lake and a few miles more to our cabin. Two days. Except the trail was riddled with huge deadfalls from several years' worth of weather. Climbing over, crawling under, or working our way around these mean obstructions was tough going, even with packs lightened due to consumed rations and beverages. Sweating, covered with bug bites, scratched, and covered with mud. The good life as always. After about ten miles, Amy sat down on a small level spot on the trail and started crying. Bonzo joined her. I was about in tears myself as I set up the tent. We had some snacks and a little Jim Beam mixed with creek water, then went to sleep.

Or tried to. Elk went crashing by our tent all night; the fabric vibrated with their pounding hooves. Fine spot we'd chosen here. Daylight mercifully came what seemed like years later and we trudged to the divide and collapsed, sleeping yesterday's troubles off beneath a hot summer sun. Thankfully, the rest of the hike was predictable, boring, and all downhill. We dropped our gear at the cabin, fed and watered Bonzo, and then piled into the Landcruiser and raced to the Wilderness Bar for double cheeseburgers, onion rings, and numerous rounds of beer and whiskey. We were soon happily drunk, and having a grand time. Home again.

That was more than twenty years ago and still the best fishing I've ever experienced on the South Fork. One day last summer, a friend and I rafted the river below Spotted Bear Ranger Station a few miles above Hungry Horse. The float was only a few miles and water conditions were ideal. Low and clear. A slight breeze and temperatures in the upper seventies. Large, billowy clouds wandered by overhead. I tied on a black Woolly Bugger, as did my friend, and we pounded the banks, worked around submerged boulders, and dredged down through deep, aquamarine seams of current.

Cutthroat came out of every holding spot, tagging our streamers and racing for cover. Brightly colored, firm and full of fight, the trout averaged fifteen inches and ran to eighteen or so. Dozens of fish, and I was happy to find that this river was still hanging in there despite the dam, obscene logging practices sanctioned by the Forest Service, and the intense fishing pressure created by an out-of-control float trip industry in the Flathead Valley. Maybe there would still be fish swimming in here ten years from now.

On the last run of the drift, I sank a large Bugger down through a deep hole. Something large hammered it and ran downstream. We beached the raft, and I got out and played the fish until it tired and could be pulled to shore. A bull trout. Maybe eight pounds and already starting to light up like a brook trout as it took on the trappings of spawning coloration. Marvelous fish. Simply marvelous. I slowly revived the creature, holding it by the tail until it casually powered off out of sight.

Still some damn good water, and I was reminded of a time on that earlier trip with Amy when we stopped so I could work a good stretch of the river. When I returned, there was a bottle of Cuervo Gold sitting on a log, and two icy margaritas nearby.

"What the hell," I thought, and Amy smiled her demon grin and said she'd run into a couple of outfitters moving a camp for some midwestern tourists. Somehow she divined that booze was part of the cargo and, as only she could, wrangled a bottle of tequila, mix, limes, and even some ice out of the two riders. The pair never had a chance. I knew this firsthand.

The drinks tasted like heaven, and the rest of the bottle died a happy death. Then we made love by the rushing river. Just two young friends high on tequila, life, and the big joke we were part of. A great day, one I'll always remember. And sometimes I still miss Amy; I'd like to go back into the wilderness and fish the South Fork with her once more for old time's sake, and maybe a little more.

Maybe for just a few days, pretend I'm young again.

Conclusion: Not Fade Away

*A*s I go around the bend, the Livingston Range slides into view. Pure white snow covers the mountains all the way down into the forest. The larch, which were blazing golden just a couple of weeks ago, are needleless, bare, gray sticks bending back and forth in the cold wind whipping down from British Columbia. The sky is a harsh blue background for isolated puffs of cloud riding swiftly up and over the Continental Divide and out onto the high, empty plains beyond.

Below me the North Fork is a much smaller river than the one I fished for big bull trout in July. Ice-cold, blue-green, and lonely, this is as good a spot as any to pull over, scramble a hundred feet or so down the steep bank and start casting for whatever might be swimming in this deep stretch of water—cutthroat, or a stray bull trout.

Sitting on the tailgate, I pull on my wool sweater, deciding to fish only what is easily reached with short, simple casts not far from shore. The sun is out and the temperature nears fifty. I remember a visit here earlier when I took a nice trout. Thoughts of other trips rise up around me and overlap each other. Any year fishing in Montana is a good one, whether you catch any trout or not. And there were some nice fish along the way: the big browns in the Clark Fork and Beaverhead, the rainbows of the Gallatin and Big Spring Creek, and the grayling in the Big Hole.

In addition to the thirteen rivers I worked in the past months, there are dozens of others around the state that are just as much fun and hold plenty of trout. The selection for this book was arbitrary and highly selective. With so much water, you have to stop somewhere.

Remembering experiences on rivers always brings back the sensations of the fishing—the bite of the wind, the pull of a fish, the smell of a pine forest, the crystal feel of cold water when I reach for a trout before me. Those and other memories make the long, dark winter bearable, barely. In February I am usually out in the back yard puffing on a cigar, clad in jeans, t-shirt, and snowshoes, casting toward an imaginary rise below a pile of snow in the driveway. The neighbors are used to this behavior by now and normally look the other way or head into town for a warm drink at the local tavern. They realize that the arcane activity will pass in an hour or so.

By midwinter an overall impression of the past year's angling develops. I know I will remember this one fondly, but there is now a disturbing aspect to the fishing that grows with intensity each season. No matter where you go, despite the fact that in many cases the fishing is better now than, say, twenty years ago, you do not have to look very long or hard to see that every single river is threatened in some way. There is logging along the North Fork, mining near the Clark Fork, development on the Gallatin, drawdown from irrigation at the Beaverhead, overcrowding on the Bighorn. The situation needs to be addressed, because rivers can be destroyed in a year or less.

Tough times and even tougher decisions await all of us who love to fish and who love rivers. Even in the vast openness and apparent emptiness of Montana, problems are pushing in from every direction. More time and money are needed from the fly fishing community to protect and preserve Montana's trout waters, which are the best in the world, period. The days of childhood when all I needed were some worms, a cheap rod and reel, a bobber, and a creek full of redhorse are long gone, and the dreaded "trout polemics" surface once again as they seem to do with frightening frequency these days.

But now the rod is rigged and the waders adjusted (there is something vaguely disturbing about all of the stuff fly fishers wear to pursue their quarry, but that's the subject of another book), and I ride a small wave of gravel and dirt down to the river. Stepping in the North Fork, I find the coolness of the river surprising. This water is really cold, but I begin casting into a deep run all the same.

Nothing happens, but the exercise and the sight of the dead drift of the line and large streamer are enjoyable. Out of the wind and in the sun the day turns pleasant, and casting becomes rhythmic. There are deer moving along a meadow across from me, and a Stellar's jay flashes dark blue and black as it makes a tremendous racket in some pines along the bank.

Perhaps a smaller tippet and a nymph would turn the trick. The fish aren't buying the streamer action and nothing is coming off the river. Opting for the delicate approach also means the addition of a twist-on a few inches above the fly. A bunch of offerings with this outfit fail to excite a trout, so the routine shifts to auto-pilot. My mind drifts back into those rugged valleys leading into Glacier National Park heartland. Walking or daydreaming, you can spend a lifetime back in there.

The rod is almost jerked from my hand and the line starts running directly across the stream. Could this be a bull trout lately moving back downriver? The fight plays long and deep like a bull, and I work the fish cautiously, trying to ease it out of the stronger current and toward shore. Each time the struggle appears to be nearing a conclusion the fish bolts for deep water, causing the drag to buzz and bending the rod double. This goes on for some time, and I am beginning to regret bringing the four-weight instead of something more authoritarian. The leader is doomed, I know with certainty.

Finally, the running in the river ends. There is only a strong, unmoving force at the end of the line. I can see the shadow of the fish as it sulks, dead still in the water. I walk back toward the bank, pulling the fish with me. Line, almost all of it, returns to the reel. The fish is in the shallows, motionless. I think, "What a way to end the year, with a big bull trout taken on a nymph."

But this is not a bull trout. I can see this clearly now that the fish is out of the flickering currents that bend and distort the light and my vision. This is not a westslope cutthroat trout of epic proportions, either.

Hell no! At the end of the line is a trophy whitefish. The damn thing is at least a couple of rippling pounds of scaly brown, silver, and white. The nymph is hooked in the thing's suckerlike lips, which are opening and closing in a steady puckering motion. I am transported back to my college days, but only briefly. I had no idea these fish could be so strong. The whitefish is the largest I've ever caught. A classic. Where's the first tee and what's the course record? And did anybody remember to bring the Everclear and White Owls? This fish deserves a toast of refined dimensions.

A lunker whitefish. I'd better alert the media. They will be interested. This is hot stuff. A perfect conclusion to a curious season.

Notes and Comments

For many of us a good deal of the fun associated with any adventure revolves around the various aspects of planning the extravaganza. All the same, the following are only the briefest of suggestions concerning guides, outfitters, and places to stay and eat, along with a few sources of information.

All of the information is based on my somewhat limited experience in the state. Just because some operation is not mentioned does not mean that I do not consider it worthwhile or wonderful. I just do not know anything about the person, place, or thing. So, for those who are not mentioned, please forego the obscene phone calls and letter bombs!

Montana in General

The state of Montana has one of the best promotion departments in the country. Travel Montana (800-847-4868 out of state and 444-2654 in-state; internet, http://travel.mt.gov/) publishes a couple of excellent booklets that point travelers in many appropriate directions. Ask for the current editions of the *Montana Travel Planner, Montana Vacation Guide,* and state highway map. There is sufficient information in these sources concerning guides, outfitters, hotels, motels, and campgrounds to set up a fishing excursion anywhere in the state.

Off the Beaten Path (27 E. Main, Bozeman 59715; telephone 406-586-1311), run by Bill and Pam Bryan, will plan a trip itinerary based on your desires and needs and the amount of money you wish to spend. Their fee for this service is a percentage of the total trip cost. The firm has a good reputation in the region.

As for clothing, even in July there can be snow, so pack for spring, summer, and fall weather, including rain gear. Good sunglasses, insect repellent, and hiking boots are necessities.

A nine-foot rod that can handle six- and seven-weight lines—floating, intermediate, and sinking—is a prime choice. After this, a three-weight and a five-weight are nice selections. Bring both chest and hip waders along with stream cleats for places like Rock Creek. Buy your patterns locally.

Licenses cost $45 per season and $10 for two days for non-residents. Most waters are open all year, but many have special catch-and-release seasons with artificial lures only that run from December 1 through the third Saturday in May, when the general season opens. Pick up a copy of the Montana Fishing Regulations when you purchase your license.

Kootenai River

The Kootenai Angler (13846 Hwy. 37, Libby 59923; telephone 406-293-7578), a guide service run by Dave Blackburn, costs $175 per day for one or two anglers. Blackburn also operates a fly shop that will handle your needs. Also, Linehan Outfitting Company, 472 Upper Ford Road, Troy, MT 59935; telephone 406-295-4872.

Libby Area Chamber of Commerce: 905 W. 9th St., Box 704, 59923; telephone 406-293-3832.

North Fork of the Flathead River

Lakestream Fly Fishers (15 Central Avenue, Whitefish 59937; telephone 406-862-1298) is run by George Widener. This shop has everything an angler will need, and George will guide trips down the river. Grouse Mountain Lodge (Hwy. 93 & Fairway Drive, Whitefish 59937; telephone 800-621-1802 or 862-3000 in-state) has rooms starting at $77, along with a restaurant and lounge. The Whitefish Lake Restaurant (telephone 406-862-5285), just across the highway, has good food.

Whitefish Chamber of Commerce: 525 E. 3rd St., 59937; telephone 406-862-3501.

St. Mary River

Joe Kipp (Morning Star Outfitters, Box 968, Browning 59417; telephone 406-338-2785) knows the fishing on the Blackfeet Reservation intimately and is a good guy with whom to spend a few days fishing around here. Rates are around $200 per day. Tribal licenses cost $7.50 per day and $40 for the season. A Montana license is also required.

The War Bonnet Lodge (Jct. 2 & Hwy. 89, Browning 59417; telephone 406-338-7610) has rooms for around $40 per night and a cafe.

Blackfeet Tribal Offices: telephone 406-338-7806 for further travel information.

Bitterroot River

The Lodge is located on an isolated stretch of the Bitterroot; telephone 406-363-4615. Cost is around $450 per day and includes everything.

Bitterroot Valley Chamber of Commerce: 105 E. Main St., Hamilton 59840; telephone 406-363-6518.

Rock Creek and Clark Fork River

Grizzly Hackle (215 W. Front, Missoula 59802; telephone 800-297-8996) has an excellent reputation in the area and can provide you with anything you might need for fishing. The Missoula area is loaded with quality hotels, motels, bed and breakfast inns, and fine restaurants. The Depot restaurant (telephone 406-728-7007) is a good choice.

Missoula Area Chamber of Commerce: 825 E. Front St., Box 7577, Missoula 59808; telephone 406-543-6623 or 800-526-3405.

Big Hole River and Beaverhead River

Tim Tollett at Frontier Anglers (Box 11, Dillon 59725; telephone 800-228-5263) and Robert Butler Outfitting Company (Box 303, Twin Bridges 59754; telephone 406-684-5773) float both rivers for around $250 per day for two anglers. Frontier also puts out an excellent catalog. (One word of caution: If you plan to fish the Beaverhead with serious intent, do not go out on the town with either Tollett or his guide, Tim Mosolf. Your reflexes the next day will be somewhat diminished.)

Beaverhead County Chamber of Commerce: Box 830, Dillon 59725; telephone 406-683-5511.

Gallatin River

The Lone Mountain Guest Ranch (Box 69, Big Sky 59716; telephone 406-995-4644) is one of the nicest in the state. In addition to guiding on the Gallatin for $175 for two per day, the ranch offers complete family vacations along with float trips on other rivers, float tube fishing, horsepack trips, and angling instruction. Another place to stay and eat is Buck's T-4 Lodge (Box 279, Big Sky 59716; telephone 800-822-4484 or 995-4111 in-state). The menu here includes such unusual items as West Texas antelope. The lodge is just yards from the river.

Bozeman Area Chamber of Commerce: Box B, 1205 E. Main St., Bozeman 59715; telephone 406-586-5421or 800-228-4224.

Bighorn River

There are several quality outfitters and guides located in Fort Smith (zip code 59035). Among them are Quill Gordon Fly Fishers (Box 597; telephone 406-666-2253) and Bighorn River Lodge (Box

756; telephone 800-235-5450). Hardin is about forty-five miles from Fort Smith by Road 313 and is a good place to stay. The Lariat Motel (709 North Center Ave., Hardin 59034; telephone 406-665-2683) is comfortable.

Hardin Area Chamber of Commerce: 219 North Center Ave., Hardin 59034; telephone 406-665-1672.

Musselshell River

To date I have not run across anyone who guides on this piece of water, so you are on your own. The Graves Motel (Box 772, 106 S. Central, Harlowton 59036; telephone 406-632-5855) is cheap and has a bar and restaurant. The Crazy Mountain Inn (100 Main, Martinsdale 59053; telephone 406-572-3307) offers food and lodging. The Mint, right across the road, provides evening beverages.

Harlowton Chamber of Commerce: Box 694, Harlowton 59036; telephone 406-632-4694.

Big Spring Creek

Fly Fisher's Retreat (825 8th Ave. S., Great Falls 59405; telephone 406-453-9192) has two-day trips for $200 per day with a minimum of two anglers. The price includes transportation from Great Falls, breakfast, two lunches, dinner, and one night's lodging. The operation also has a complete fly shop. For those on their own, there is the Yogo Inn (Box 939, 211 E. Main, Lewistown 59457; telephone 406-538-8721 or 800-860-YOGO) for about $40 per night. There is also a restaurant, coffee shop, and lounge. Don's Western Outdoor (120 2nd Ave. S., Box 780, Lewistown 59457; telephone 406-538-9408) has fly fishing equipment and licenses.

Lewistown Area Chamber of Commerce: Box 818, Lewistown 59457; telephone 406-538-5436 or 800-216-5436.

Missouri River

There are numerous guides and outfitters on this river. One I have had extensive experience with is Pro Outfitters (Box 621, Helena 59601; telephone 406-442-5489 or 800-858-3497), run by Paul Roos, who is knowledgeable and personable. Cost is around $250 per day per boat for two. Extended floats are available. Finding a place to stay and eat in Helena, Great Falls, Townsend, or along the river is no problem.

Great Falls Area Chamber of Commerce: 815 2nd St., Box 2127, Great Falls 59403; telephone 406-761-4434.

Helena Area Chamber of Commerce: 225 Cruse Ave., Suite A, Helena 59601; telephone 406-442-4120 or 800-7HELENA.

Glasgow Chamber of Commerce (for the river below Fort Peck Dam): Box 832, 59230; telephone 406-228-2222.

Further Reading

The following titles might add some further information to the Montana experience.

McClane's New Standard Fishing Encyclopedia, edited by A. J. McClane, contains a little bit about just about everything associated with fishing (Holt, Rinehart and Winston, 1974).

Nymph Fishing for Larger Trout by Charles E. Brooks is the definitive text on nymphing techniques (Crown Publishers, 1976).

The Complete Book of Western Hatches by Rick Hafele and Dave Hughes contains some good information on the major species in Montana (Frank Amato Publications, 1981).

Roadside Geology of Montana by David Alt and Donald W. Hyndman gives the average bozo a pretty fair idea of what took place with the landscape in Montana (Mountain Press Publishing Company, 1986).

A River Runs Through It and Other Stories by Norman Maclean is one of the best books about fishing ever written, and all of the events take place in Montana (University of Chicago Press, 1976).

English Creek by Ivan Doig gives a glimpse of an earlier version of Montana east of the Rockies (Penguin, 1985).

Blood Sport by Robert F. Jones has absolutely nothing to do with fishing in Montana but is required reading for all serious anglers (Simon and Schuster, 1974).

Ghost Towns of Montana by Donald C. Miller is great reading with plenty of anecdotes and firsthand reports dealing with the state's wild past (Pruett Publishing Company, 1974).

Montana Fly Fishing Guide–East and *Montana Fly Fishing Guide–West* by John Holt. Thanks to Stan and Glenda Bradshaw and Gary La Fontaine, these two books are definitive (Greycliff Publishing Company, 1996).

Index

(Photograph by Ginny Diers)

John Holt is the author of numerous books on fly fishing, including *Waist Deep in Montana's Lakes, Reel Deep in Montana's Rivers, Montana Fly Fishg Guide–East,* and *Montana Fly Fishing Guide–West.* His many fly fishing essays and articles have appeared in *Fly Fisherman, Field & Stream, Fly Rod & Reel, Gray's Sporting Journal,* and other outdoor sports journals. He lives, writes, and fly fishes in Montana.